Laura Ingalls Wilder

Laura Ingalls Wilder

Storyteller of the Prairie

Ginger Wadsworth

Lerner Publications Company • Minneapolis

To Margie and to other parents
who make time to read to their children

The author traveled to many Laura Ingalls Wilder sites around the country to complete her research. She would like to thank the following people and organizations for their help: The Laura Ingalls Wilder Memorial Society, Pepin, WI, Wllma Kurtis at the Little House on the Prairie Site, Independence, KS; Laura and Almanzo Wilder Association, Malone, NY; Shirley Knakmuhs at the Laura Ingalls Wilder Museum, Walnut Grove, MN; Laura Ingalls Wilder Park and Museum, Burr Oak, IA; Mary Jo Dathe at the Laura Ingalls Wilder Site, Spring Valley, MN; Vivian Glover at the Laura Ingalls Memorial Society, De Smet, SD; Jean Coday and staff at the Laura Ingalls Wilder-Rose Wilder Lane Home and Museum, Mansfield, MO; Dwight Miller, Pat Wildenberg, and staff at the Herbert Hoover Library, West Branch, IA; Bill Wadsworth, research assistant, and Susan Breckner Rose, my editor.

Lerner Publications Company
A division of Lerner Publishing Group
241 First Avenue North
Minneapolis, MN 55401 U.S.A.

Website address: www.lernerbooks.com

Library of Congress Cataloging-in-Publication Data

Wadsworth, Ginger.
    Laura Ingalls Wilder : storyteller of the Prairie / Ginger Wadsworth.
        p.   cm.
    Includes bibliographical references and index.
    Summary: Tells the life story of the author of the "Little House" books from her childhood in Wisconsin to her death at Rocky Ridge Farm at the age of ninety.
    ISBN 0-8225-4950-6 (lib. bdg. : alk. paper)
    1. Wilder, Laura Ingalls, 1867–1957—Biography—Juvenile literature. 2. Women authors, American—20th century— Biography—Juvenile literature. 3. Children's stories—Authorship— Juvenile literature. 4. Frontier and pioneer life—Juvenile literature. [1. Wilder, Laura Ingalls, 1867–1957. 2. Authors, American. 3. Women—Biography. 4. Frontier and pioneer life.] I. Title.
PS3545.I342Z92   1997
813'.52—dc20
    [B]   96-6273

Manufactured in the United States of America
3 4 5 6 7 8 – JR – 08 07 06 05 04 03

Contents

Garth Williams drew Laura and her family walking through the Big Woods near their little house.

ONE

Pioneer Girl

1867–1872

After feeding the chickens and setting the bread out to rise in the kitchen, Laura Ingalls Wilder sat down at her desk. She picked up a pencil. Slipping back in time, she started to write down her memories of when she had been a pioneer girl.

"Out in the meadow," Laura wrote, "I picked a wild sunflower, and as I looked into its golden heart, such a wave of homesickness came over me that I almost wept. I wanted Mother, with her gentle voice and quiet firmness; I longed to hear Father's jolly songs and to see his twinkling blue eyes."

Memories came flooding back to Laura—the log cabin in the Big Woods of Wisconsin, the trips by covered wagon to Indian country and the prairie with her sisters, her marriage to Almanzo Wilder. Now both Ma and Pa were gone and so was much of the frontier.

Laura believed that her pioneer stories "were much too good to be lost." She would write her memoirs for her daughter, Rose. Over the next few months, Laura filled the pages of a tablet of blue-lined paper. When she was done, she wrote "Pioneer Girl" at the top of the first page.

Laura mailed the manuscript to her daughter, who was a famous writer in New York. Maybe the stories would help Rose with the frontier fiction she was writing.

Rose showed "Pioneer Girl" to an editor at a New York publishing house. With Rose's advice, and that of an editor, Laura rewrote and retitled her book, combining some of Pa's stories with her own memories of life in Wisconsin. Harper and Brothers publishing company liked her new story.

Little House in the Big Woods, a book for young readers with illustrations by Helen Sewell, was published in 1932. Laura was sixty-five.

She thought that this book would end her writing career. To her surprise, children wrote to her, "begging for more" about the Ingalls family and pioneer life. Laura told a reporter that she "was amazed because I didn't know how to write. I went to 'Little red schoolhouses' all over the west and I was never graduated from anything."

Once again, she relied on her keen memory and story-telling skills. She started a second book, about Almanzo's boyhood on a farm in upstate New York, then a third, about living on the prairie . . . and a fourth. . . .

Laura's Pa was Charles Philip Ingalls. He was born in 1836 in New York. His parents, like many others at that time, were pioneers. They moved west to Illinois, then north, where they settled in Wisconsin Territory, near the village of Concord. Wisconsin became a state in 1848.

Charles had eight brothers and sisters. The boys learned to hunt and trap in the woods. They worked on their own farm and hired themselves out to other farms. If they had time, the children went to school. Charles knew that it was important to be able to write and read. He also learned to play the violin. Charles could sing and dance, and everyone loved to listen to his music at weddings, parties, house-raisings, and family gatherings.

Laura's Ma was Caroline Lake Quiner. Born in 1839, Caroline helped her mother with the six younger children and with the cooking, sewing, and gardening. She also attended school. A plain-looking, gentle girl, Caroline loved to read and, in her spare time, wrote poetry and essays. Her mother had been a teacher and stressed the importance of education, even on the edge of the frontier.

After several moves, the Quiners had settled in Wisconsin near the Ingallses. The Ingalls and Quiner children became friends as they were growing up. Charles and Caroline met frequently when the frontier families gathered to attend church, go on sleigh rides, and hold spelling bees and dances.

Just after her sixteenth birthday, Caroline passed the teacher's examination. She taught two terms at the school where she had studied. Although quiet, she was a good teacher. She shared her pay—about three dollars a week—with her family.

After courting for several years, Charles and Caroline were married in 1860. Each brought different traits to their marriage. Charles, with his sparkling blue eyes and unruly brown hair and beard, had a restless spirit and a need to "move on." Caroline wanted to create a home and raise well-mannered, educated children.

Three years after their marriage, they moved to a log cabin in the rolling hills of western Wisconsin, near the Mississippi River town of Pepin. Their first child, Mary Amelia, was born on January 10, 1865, in the Big Woods of Wisconsin. Laura Elizabeth Ingalls was born on February 7, 1867.

ρ

Caroline Lake Quiner and Charles Ingalls were married in 1860.

When Mary and Laura were five and three, Pa loaded up the covered wagon and moved the family west to the state of Kansas. Prairie, not forest, lay beyond the Mississippi River. Pa was tired of cutting trees in the Big Woods and plowing the root-laden soil.

The Ingalls family settled southwest of Independence, a brand-new town. Pa found 160 acres to homestead. According to the United States government, when the family had lived on the land for five years, farmed it, and built a house, the 160 acres would belong to them.

Pa started to build a house. It had four walls of logs, notched at the ends. The canvas wagon top fit over the skeleton roof of slender saplings. There were square spaces for windows but no glass yet. The floor was hard-packed prairie dirt. When the house was finished, Pa and Ma carried in clothes, dishes, quilts, Pa's fiddle, and Ma's books from the wagon. Laura felt right at home.

Pa hung one of Ma's patchwork quilts over the door opening. He promised to build a stout oak door with a latch before winter. He told Ma, "We're going to do well here, Caroline. This is a country I'll be contented to stay in the rest of my life."

"Even when it's settled up?" Ma asked.

"Even when its settled up."

Laura felt the same contentment as Pa. She liked being outside under the big blue sky, running barefoot through the high prairie grass, watching the birds and rabbits, and letting the mud on the creek bottom ooze between her toes.

When she was out of Ma's sight, Laura often slipped off her bonnet to feel the sun on her face. Mary, on the other hand, refused to let her silky blond hair blow in the harsh wind, and she scolded Laura.

Laura and Mary helped set the table with tin dishes and utensils, brought in wood for the fireplace, and made the beds. Like Ma, Mary was quiet and enjoyed working in the cabin. But Laura would keep looking out a door or window, watching the prairie from sunrise to sunset.

Every day, Pa was busy. Over the next few weeks, he dug a well, built a barn, and plowed the rich dark soil. On some days, he helped new neighbors build their log cabins.

In the evenings, Laura and Mary begged Pa to play his fiddle. Laura never tired of hearing songs like "Home Sweet Home" and "Auld Lang Syne." As he played, Pa tapped his foot to the beat. Sometimes he sang. His clear, deep voice reminded Laura of the sound of a bell. Later on, from the trundle bed she shared with Mary, Laura watched the moonlight filter through the canvas roof and between the cracks in the logs.

One day Laura discovered a faint trail in the grass. It passed right by the Ingalls cabin and disappeared into the prairie. She asked Pa where the trail went.

Pa explained that they had homesteaded on an Indian reservation. The land belonged to the Osage Indians who had been away on a hunting trip when the Ingallses first arrived on the high grassy prairie. Now the Osage were back, living in several camps along the nearby Verdigris River. They used the trail every day.

Sometimes women and children passed by on ponies. The ponies didn't have bridles or saddles; the children did not always wear clothes. Laura wished she could be an Indian child on a pony instead of a "young lady." She wanted to race across the prairie in the sun, letting her long brown hair blow free in the wind.

She kept her "naughty" thoughts to herself. Mary wouldn't understand. Neither would Ma, who did not like the Indians and wished they would keep to themselves. Pa told Ma that the Indians were friendly. He often met them in the woods along the river where he hunted.

At first, Pa was right. The Osage were friendly and

Pa took Laura and Mary to see an Osage village near the Ingalls cabin in Kansas.

stopped unexpectedly at the cabin. Several times, they came inside. They spoke their own language, so Laura didn't know what they were saying. While Ma fed them cornmeal, Laura stared. The Indians wore beaded leather moccasins and skunk furs. They tied their hair with colored string and feathers.

One hot day in August, Pa walked Laura and Mary to the Osage village, but the Indians were away hunting. Laura saw the ashes from their campfires and holes in the ground from the tent poles. Laura and Mary collected colored beads in the dust.

When they returned home, they learned that Ma had given birth to another daughter. A neighbor, Mrs. Scott, had helped with the delivery. Ma and Pa named the baby Caroline Celestia Ingalls and decided to call her Carrie. Ma wrote the baby's name and birth date, August 3, 1870, in the family Bible below Mary and Laura's birth records.

That fall and winter, as more and more settlers arrived and homesteaded on the Osage hunting land, the Indians grew disturbed and talked of war. At night, Laura heard Indian war chants over the howls of the wolves.

In the spring of 1871, when Laura was four, Ma and Pa decided to return to Wisconsin. The man who had bought their farm there could no longer make the payments. They could reclaim their old log house in the woods and not have to worry about the Osage Indians.

Once again, Ma and Pa packed the covered wagon. As they started east, Laura peered west. Jack, their bulldog, trailed behind the wagon, following the ruts in the road. Laura watched as the tall prairie grass seemed to swallow up their snug log house.

Several weeks later, the covered wagon rumbled past the town of Pepin, Wisconsin. Pa turned northeast to the Big Woods. Laura saw a split rail fence and, in a clearing, a little cabin. They were home.

Everyone seemed to have something special to do, except Laura. By sunrise each day, Pa was off with his ax to clear more land so he could plant wheat. On other days, he headed into the woods to hunt and set traps. Ma fussed over the house, washing windows and scrubbing the floors.

For the first time, Mary went to school, leaving Laura at home with Ma and Carrie. Laura missed Mary. Carrie was too little to play with dolls or climb trees with Laura. The best part of the day was the afternoon, when she walked partway down the dirt road to meet Mary on her way home.

Sometimes relatives and friends stopped by in the evenings to visit, and Pa would play his fiddle. They sang or danced to tunes like "Dixie" and "Sweet Betsy from Pike." Laura liked to watch the ladies' dresses swish and the men's boots strike the floor.

Mary and Laura loved to watch and listen to Pa play his fiddle.

When Pa wasn't too tired from working in the fields, Laura and Mary begged him for a story. "Voice in the Woods" was scary, but Laura loved it. She had heard the story so many times that she knew it word-for-word. They also played games. Laura's favorite was "mad dog," when Pa crawled on the floor, growling and shaking his shaggy beard. On quieter evenings, Mary played with her rag doll. Laura dressed Susan, a corncob doll, in a handkerchief. Jack and Black Susan, the cat, dozed nearby. Ma often read a story from *Wonders of the Animal World,* a chapter from a novel, or a passage from the Bible. Most books were borrowed from the school or from neighbors.

All summer long, Mary went to school and Laura stayed at home with Carrie. Dust stirred through the air, and weeks passed without rain. By the summer's end, brush crackled underfoot and a nearby creek dried up. Once, a forest fire broke out nearby. Fortunately, the hot winds pushed the flames away from the house.

In October it was still hot and dry in the Big Woods. Laura didn't care. All she could think about was school. That fall she walked with Mary and their older cousins along the wagon road to the Barry Corner School. The sisters shared a shiny lunch pail and one schoolbook. Laura was not yet five, but she loved school, especially reading and writing. There she also got to play with her cousins and the children of Ma and Pa's friends.

During the winter months, when Laura and Mary could not reach school because snowdrifts blocked the roads, Ma helped her daughters keep up with their lessons. She also taught them to embroider and sew. Under Ma's watchful eye, Laura learned to make neat stitches.

The house filled with aunts, uncles, and cousins on

Christmas Day. There were red mittens and a stick of red-striped peppermint candy for each cousin. Pa had built a shelf for Ma, with carved flowers, leaves, a star, and a moon. He hung the shelf between the windows, and Ma put her china shepherdess, with her china curls and bonnet, on the shelf.

Laura unwrapped a new rag doll, which she immediately named Charlotte. She had "a face of white cloth with black button eyes. A black pencil had made her eyebrows, and her cheeks and mouth were red with the ink made from poke-berries. Her hair was black yarn that had been knit and raveled, so that it was curly.

"She had little red flannel stockings and little black cloth gaiters for shoes, and her dress was pretty pink and blue calico." It was a Christmas Laura never forgot.

Garth Williams drew the Ingalls family arriving at their dugout on Plum Creek.

~~~ TWO ~~~

On Plum Creek

1872–1875

For two years, Pa produced several fine crops of wheat, but his traps in the woods were often empty. Wagons were rolling past their house, filled with families who wanted to settle in the Big Woods. Pa dreamed about moving to a place where there were fewer people. Laura knew Pa had an "itchy foot."

When Laura was seven, Ma and Pa packed the covered wagon, and the Ingalls family started toward western Minnesota. Day by day, Pa followed faint wagon trails west. Laura peeked out from the canvas cover. There was so much to see—flocks of birds, spring wildflowers, and always, miles and miles of green grass.

At night the Ingallses camped off the trail, usually along a little creek. Ma cooked dinner over the campfire. Because Laura was so short, she stood on a wooden box to help wash the dishes at the camp table.

One night Laura heard a strange noise. Ma explained that it was a train whistle. Pa added that a train traveled farther in a day than an ox team could travel in a week. Laura couldn't believe it.

Peering out from the wagon the next day, she saw her

first train. Big and black, the train seemed to rush across the prairie. Long puffs of dark smoke streamed back from the engine. Pa spoke firmly to the horses so they wouldn't spook.

After weeks of travel, the Ingallses reached the small village of Walnut Grove in southwestern Minnesota. Pa bought 172 acres of grassy prairie along Plum Creek.

Pa stopped the wagon on a bluff above Plum Creek. He told Ma and the girls that a dugout, a house built into the earth, came with the land. Laura looked everywhere for her new home. Finally, she spotted a door in the grassy embankment. The dugout, carved into the bluff like a cave, lay behind the door. It was the same size as the wagon bed. Thick, tall prairie grass grew on the roof.

While Ma cleaned the tiny dugout, Laura began to unpack the wagon. Mary looked after Carrie. Just before dusk, Laura helped Pa carry willow boughs inside and spread them on the floor so they wouldn't have to sleep on the dirt. That first night in the dugout, Laura missed the sound of the wind blowing through the wagon top and wondered when she would get used to sleeping inside again.

Each morning after breakfast, Laura made her bed and did the dishes. She filled her little pail with fresh water from Plum Creek and carried it back to the dugout. She and Mary helped Ma air the straw-filled mattresses in the sun. Mary would rather read or sew, but Laura hated to sit still.

In the thickets by the creek, Mary and Laura picked plums. Jack kept them company while they worked. Laura ate the juiciest plums while she filled her pail. Picking fruit was more like play than work. Later, Ma showed them how to spread the plums on clean cloths to dry in the sun. During the winter, they would eat the dried plums.

When their chores were done, Laura and Mary played.

Farmers like Pa plowed the rolling prairie with a team of oxen.

They gathered bouquets of blue flag iris for Ma and made necklaces from the rushes along the edge of the creek. Sometimes they climbed above the dugout to the prairie. They waved at Pa in the distance as he turned over the sod with a plow pulled by a team of oxen.

When Laura and Mary started school in Walnut Grove, Laura was almost eight. To get to school, they waded across Plum Creek, careful not to splash their newly ironed calico dresses. They walked beside the dusty wagon road on the grass so their feet wouldn't get dirty. Most of the students were homesteaders, like Laura and Mary, but a few were town children. Some of the students brought schoolbooks from home. Laura and Mary shared Ma's old books, from her days as a teacher. One was a speller, another was a reader, and the third covered arithmetic.

The creamery was one of the many new businesses in Walnut Grove.

The town of Walnut Grove was growing. On the way home from school, Laura watched the ongoing construction of Union Congregational Church. After it was finished, the Ingalls family rode to church in the wagon every Sunday. Although Laura often fidgeted during the long sermons, she liked to sing hymns and memorize Bible passages. She borrowed books from the church library to take home and read.

In December the townspeople dedicated the church building with an evening Christmas party. While the congregation sang hymns, Laura's mind and eyes were on the decorated Christmas tree in the front of the church—the first one she had ever seen. Everyone received gifts, donated by churches back east. Laura got a fur cape and muff, along with a tiny china jewel box.

Following the long Minnesota winter, everyone welcomed spring. Pa planted wheat. While it was growing, he decided to build a real house with smooth, sawed pine boards and glass windows.

Every day Laura and Mary hurried through their chores in the dugout, then raced to "the wonderful house." Sometimes they hung wood shavings over their ears, like earrings. "Laura tucked long ones in her hair and they hung down in golden curls, just the colour she had always wanted her hair to be."

Laura and Mary watched Pa nail shingles on the roof. While he worked, Laura peered through the real glass windows, and opened and closed the store-bought doors with white china knobs.

When they moved in, Laura shared the attic with Mary. Laura loved the feel of the smooth boards under her bare feet and the piney smell of the wood. It was wonderful to be in a house where so much warm sunshine poured through each window.

Before long, it would be time to cut the wheat. The plants were almost as tall as Pa. Looking out at the wheat fields, Laura saw "silky, shimmery green rippling over a curve of the prairie. . . . and all around it the wild prairie grasses looked coarser and darker green."

Like everyone else in the family, Laura dreamed about what the money from the wheat crop would bring—new boots for Pa and new shoes for her and Mary. Ma would have woven cloth to sew into dresses.

Marcy Dunn Ramsey drew Laura fending off grasshoppers that destroyed crops across Minnesota in 1875.

❧ THREE ❧

Plague and Hardship on the Prairie

1875–1879

One summer day, the sky darkened at noon. It was not a rainstorm, as Laura first thought. For some strange reason, Jack growled. A cloud moved across the sky faster than the wind. Laura saw the sun glitter on thin particles in the cloud. The particles were brown grasshoppers—millions of them. She shivered. The rasping sound of their beating wings filled the air.

The grasshoppers began to hit the ground. Some clung to Laura, clawing her skin and her skirt. Laura, Mary, Carrie, and Ma raced into the house. The grasshoppers struck the house like hail. Some slipped in through cracks and under doors. From inside the house, Laura heard them snip and bite everything, even the clothes on the line.

Pa surrounded the wheat fields with dozens of fires, hoping the smoke would drive the insects away. Nothing worked. Within hours, the grasshoppers had eaten the wheat, Ma's vegetable garden, the plums along the creek, leaves, grass—anything they could chew. Their bodies clogged the water in

Plum Creek. When every green thing was gone, the grasshoppers laid eggs in the ground, then left.

Across much of Minnesota, the prairie lay dry and barren. Schools closed. Businesses shut down. Many homesteaders decided to board up their homes and return to their families in the East.

One by one, covered wagons rolled out of town. Laura waved good-bye to her classmates and church friends. And she wondered if her family would move . . . again.

Pa could not find a job in Walnut Grove or in any of the other small prairie towns. Desperate for work, he decided to walk more than two hundred miles to eastern Minnesota where there were no grasshoppers. He would pick crops and tend other farmers' fields for a dollar a day.

Pa had never been away for more than a few nights at a time. Laura missed him terribly. So did Ma, Mary, and Carrie. Everyone pretended to be cheerful during the long summer.

Without Pa around, Laura and Mary did extra chores. After helping Ma with the inside work, Laura herded the cows along Plum Creek, helping them find a little water to drink or a few twigs to nibble. The bare earth felt dry and hot beneath her feet. Then she hurried inside. Laura hated to stay indoors, but because the grasshoppers had eaten all the leaves, the trees didn't provide any shade. The sun baked the land dry, causing clouds of dust to blow day and night. Outside, the cows mooed mournfully to one another because they were hungry.

At the end of the summer, Pa walked back to Walnut Grove, bringing enough money to last them through the winter. Then the rains came, soaking the hard soil and filling Plum Creek. Pa unwrapped his fiddle and played songs. Laura and Mary started school again.

On the first of November, Ma gave birth to a son. She and Pa named the baby Charles Frederick Ingalls. Every day after school, Laura and Mary hurried home to see him. Right away, the girls began calling their new brother Freddie.

Pa planted wheat in the spring. The prairie turned green, and the trees grew new leaves. Although Ma and Freddie had been sick during the long, cold winter, everyone hoped for better times.

On Sundays, Ma rested at home with Freddie and Carrie. Laura walked two and a half miles to church with Mary and Pa. The prairie was beautiful. Laura saw "the path winding ahead, flecked with sunshine and shadow and the beautiful golden-hearted daisies scattered all along the way."

The Ingalls family joined the Congregational church in Walnut Grove.

The sun warmed the prairie. Millions of green grasshoppers began to push out of eggs deposited the year before. In the wheat fields, Laura gathered handfuls of the tiny insects. They were delicate-looking now, with small wings and legs, but she knew they would grow into big, hungry brown grasshoppers.

For the second time, the grasshoppers chewed everything in their way, including the wheat, leaving the prairie bare again. Then, like an army, the grasshoppers marched west in search of more food. Laura noticed that Pa no longer sang or whistled. Ma still looked tired and thin. Laura knew they would have to move.

Once again the Ingallses packed the covered wagon. Unlike the grasshoppers, they traveled east. Jack raced about, sniffing for game. But no one was excited about "back-trailing." Pa hunched over the reins. Sitting next to him, Ma held Freddie. The baby still wasn't strong, and Ma was worried.

Like her father, Laura dreamed of open spaces and new lands in the West. But at nine and a half, she was old enough to know that they would have to live with Uncle Peter and Aunt Eliza—Pa's brother and Ma's sister—until the times improved.

That summer the two families, totaling thirteen people, shared one farmhouse in southeastern Minnesota. The cousins played in the pasture next to the Zumbro River. They ate wild plums and roasted crab apples over campfires.

Laura had lots of chores, but she especially enjoyed bringing in the cows every afternoon. She walked "along the cow paths forgetful of milking time and stern parents waiting while I gathered wild flowers, waded in the creek, watched the squirrels hastening to their homes in the tree tops and listened to the sleepy twittering of the birds."

All summer there was a sense of uneasiness. Baby Freddie was weak and sickly. On August 27, Freddie suddenly died. The Ingallses buried him nearby in South Troy, Minnesota. Ma recorded in the family Bible that Charles Frederick Ingalls was nine months old when he died.

A few weeks later, the family loaded up the wagon. Pa

Hoping for better times, the Ingalls family packed up their belongings and headed across the prairie.

had a job in Burr Oak, Iowa. For the last time, they passed the cemetery where Freddie was buried.

Days later the wagon reached Burr Oak. To Laura the town seemed old and dark, with its red brick buildings and gnarled burr oaks. But no one complained. Pa was to work with the owner of a hotel in town called the Burr Oak House.

The Ingallses moved into the crowded noisy hotel. Guests and visitors ate three large meals a day in the dining room. The hotel hosted weddings and dances. Ma helped with the laundry, cooking, and cleaning. Laura and Mary were expected to do their share, making beds, waiting tables, and watching the smaller children.

It was a sad and difficult time. Everyone missed Freddie. Ma, who was expecting a baby in the spring, was always tired. She grumbled about the bustling saloon next door. To top it all off, the three girls came down with the measles. Laura remembered that "the hotel was a noisy place to be sick in." Other children were sent in to play with the Ingalls girls so they would be exposed to the measles "to get it over with."

When Laura discovered a bullet hole in the hotel's dining room door, she was thrilled. She learned that it had been made when a young man, who was drunk, shot at his wife. Slamming the door between them, the wife escaped the bullet and her husband.

Ma decided it was time to move. For awhile, the Ingallses lived above a grocery store on the other side of the saloon. One night the saloon caught on fire. Pa rushed out to help. Laura and her sisters watched from the front windows, ready to run if the grocery store started to burn. Below them on the street, the men formed a bucket brigade from the town pump to the saloon. They passed bucket after bucket of water down the line. The last man dumped water on the flames. Eventually the saloon was saved.

Laura and Mary attended Burr Oak School. The benches and desks were made of smoothed boards. The blackboards were black painted walls. Older students, like Mary, studied upstairs. Six-year-old Carrie started downstairs with Laura. Although Laura loved to read, write, and learn about history, she struggled with her multiplication tables. It took her all spring to memorize them to the tune of "Yankee Doodle." Then she moved upstairs to study with Mary.

William Reid, their principal and teacher, was sixteen years old, the same age as Ma was when she had first taught school. An "elocutionist," he taught his students to read out loud with feeling.

For her twelfth birthday, Mary had received a book with speeches, stories, and poems, such as "Paul Revere's Ride" and "The Village Blacksmith." They were perfect to read out loud. Under Ma's supervision, Mary and Laura practiced speaking skills every afternoon in the sitting room above the grocery store. As they read from Mary's book, they were unaware of the customers who gathered regularly to listen to them recite.

For the third time in less than a year, the family moved, this time to a brick house outside of town near the oak woods. Pa bought a milk cow. Once again, Laura's favorite chore was to kick off her shoes and take the cow to the pasture each morning and fetch her in the evening.

On May 23, 1877, Ma had a baby. Ma and Pa named her Grace Pearl. Laura noticed that Grace had golden hair like Mary and bright blue eyes like Pa. They all adored the beautiful, healthy baby and believed she symbolized an end to their troubles.

Baby Grace

When she wasn't helping Ma with Grace or tending the family's vegetable garden, Laura explored the woods or nearby Burr Oak cemetery with a friend from school. She remembered that "work and play were so mixed that I could not tell them apart."

One day a neighbor named Mrs. Starr came to talk to Ma and Laura. Dr. and Mrs. Starr owned a big house and were important people in Burr Oak. Mrs. Starr knew that the Ingallses were poor. She told Ma that she missed her grown daughters, and she wondered if Laura would come to live with her and her husband. She would adopt Laura and treat her as a daughter, buy her pretty clothes and give her an education. Laura could hardly breathe as she waited for Ma's answer. To Laura's relief, Ma politely declined. Mrs. Starr went home disappointed.

That summer Pa played marching and moving songs, like "There is a Happy Land, Far, Far, Away," on his fiddle. Laura couldn't wait to go west again. After living in Burr Oak for more than a year, Ma and Pa pulled the canvas cover over the wagon and headed back to Walnut Grove. When they arrived in the fall, they were welcomed as if they had never left.

Laura, Mary, and Carrie went back to school. It was fun to see old classmates and make new friends. Laura's favorite time became the weekly spelling bees held every Friday night in the schoolhouse.

Unlike Mary, Laura was a tomboy. At recess and after school, she joined wintertime snowball fights and played baseball in the spring. Mary disapproved. She thought Laura should be more ladylike. But Laura could hardly wait to race outside with the boys. She was proud of the fact that "only one boy in school could throw faster than me, and not always."

In February 1879, Laura turned twelve. A few weeks later, Mary became sick with a high fever and chills. Her head and throat hurt. Ma cut her long blond hair to keep her cooler. The fever persisted. Everyone thought Mary was going to die. Doctors came to the house several times. They told Pa and Ma that Mary had "brain fever," or meningitis, an infection between the brain and the skull.

Finally Mary seemed to be getting better, even though she was too weak to get out of bed. As she recovered, her eyesight began to fail. Ma and Pa called the doctors again. They said that Mary had had a stroke that was destroying the nerves in her eyes. Before long, she was completely blind.

Laura loved horses and the freedom of the open prairie.

≈≈≈ FOUR ≈≈≈

To Dakota Territory

1879–1880

Laura could hardly believe that her sister was blind. Her beautiful blue eyes looked normal, and her blond hair was growing out. Mary never complained but just rocked quietly in Ma's old hickory chair by the warm stove.

Ma had dreamed of Mary becoming a teacher. Now what was to happen to her? Worry etched Pa's thin face. He had doctors' bills and other debts to pay. Hunting was poor; even cottontail rabbits were scarce. Until times improved, Pa had to rely on odd jobs to pay the bills.

Laura helped Ma with the daily chores and took care of Grace. She ran errands for neighbors and sat with their children. She gave the nickels and dimes she earned to Pa to add to his wages.

At the age of twelve and a half, Laura wasn't a child anymore. There wasn't time to run barefoot on the prairie. Mary's blindness forced Laura to grow up quickly. She tried to curb her quick tongue and be a proper young lady like Mary.

Laura promised Pa that she would become Mary's eyes. In detail, she shared her world with her sister. But sometimes it was hard to find the right words to describe a blazing red prairie sunset or the newly washed landscape after a sudden rainstorm.

One morning while doing the dishes, Laura saw a buggy ford Plum Creek. Laura told Mary about the prancing bay horse pulling the buggy and the driver, a woman in a brown sunbonnet and brown print dress. The buggy stopped, and Aunt Docia, Pa's sister, stepped down in front of the house.

Aunt Docia was going to Dakota Territory to join her husband. Uncle Hiram worked for the Chicago and Northwestern Railroad. They wanted Pa to work as a store manager for the railroad company in Dakota Territory—selling goods to the workers and keeping track of the hours the men worked on the railroad lines. The pay was fifty dollars a month, much more than Pa would ever earn in Walnut Grove. Dozens of new towns were sprouting up along the western tracks, Aunt Docia said. There were thousands of acres to homestead on the Dakota prairie. Pa's face lit up. He wanted to go west and so did Laura.

Pa decided to take the job, promising Ma that this move would be their last. Laura hurried outside to tell the news to their dog, Jack. She explained that first Pa and Jack would leave by wagon in the morning. Later, when Mary was stronger, the rest of the family would come on the train. Laura chattered about her first train ride. Instead of running in circles and barking, the old bulldog leaned his gray head against Laura's hand. While Pa packed the wagon, Jack curled up on his horse blanket, in a corner of the lean-to at the back door.

Sometime during the night, Jack died. The family buried Jack by his favorite path. Laura realized he had been too old and tired to walk all the way to Dakota Territory.

Without Pa, the next few months passed slowly for

Laura. She helped Ma run the house and take care of Mary. Finally the summer ended. It was time to leave Walnut Grove.

Wearing a freshly ironed, brown calico dress, Laura stood with Ma, Carrie, Grace, and Mary on the train platform. As the train approached, she gripped Mary's hand. "The engine's round front window glared in the sunshine like a huge eye. The smokestack flared upward to a wide top, and black smoke rolled up from it. A sudden streak of white shot up through the smoke, then the whistle screamed a long wild scream. The roaring thing came rushing straight at them all, swelling bigger and bigger, enormous, shaking everything with noise."

Somehow, they all found seats on the train. Laura wanted to bounce on them, but instead she remembered her promise

A train rushes toward the station.

to Pa and described the red velvet seats and the big glass windows to Mary. The engine whistled, and the train swayed back and forth on the tracks, taking them away from Walnut Grove. Laura told Mary about the telegraph wire that swooped between poles where it was fastened by green glass knobs. She described the grasslands, fields, farmhouses, and barns they passed.

When they reached the end of the railroad, near the Big Sioux River in Dakota Territory, the Ingalls family moved into the railroad camp. About two hundred men slept in shanties provided by the railroad company. Few had brought their wives. Ma insisted that the girls "keep to themselves" because the men were not her idea of good neighbors.

As the train tracks moved west, so did the crew and the Ingalls family. The workers hauled their equipment with them. With each move, they dismantled the store, cook house, stable, and shanties and rebuilt them on a new site. The camp eventually relocated on the edge of Silver Lake in Dakota Territory.

Early in the morning, Laura gathered water from Silver Lake in her brown jug. She often watched great triangles of wild geese descend on the sunlit water. Wind rippled the grasses at the edge of the lake and made silvery waves. Twice a day, Laura milked the cow and moved her tether so she could reach fresh grass. Laura helped Ma with the washing, ironing, and mending. Mary was happy to work inside— making beds, sewing, washing dishes, and tending to Grace.

When they finished all their chores, Laura, Mary, and Carrie walked on the warm soft grasses toward Silver Lake. It was Laura's favorite time of the day. The sisters followed old Indian trails and worn buffalo paths. Only a little time before, Pa told them, vast herds of buffalo had roamed the prairie. But by this time, most were gone, slaughtered by white hunters.

Holding her sister's arm, Laura "painted" word pictures for Mary. They picked bouquets of flaming red tiger lilies and purple buffalo bean pods to take back to Ma.

Winter set in quickly, and the railroad crew left to join their families in the East. To protect the camp from vandals, the Ingallses were hired to stay in the surveyor's house on the bank of Silver Lake. The well-built house was bigger than any Laura had ever lived in. It was stocked with flour, beans, salted meat, potatoes, and canned food, along with coal for fuel. Their closest neighbor was twelve miles away, and it was forty miles to the nearest store.

For once Laura didn't dread being cooped inside for winter. While she worked, she peered through the real glass windows to see the endless miles of snow-covered prairie. Living in the snug house and having her family close were all Laura needed.

Pa hunted for antelope, which grazed in large herds across the prairie. At the same time, he searched for a homestead, finally deciding on 160 acres about a mile from the future town of De Smet.

The winter months flew by. Laura cleaned and helped Ma cook delicious meals using the food in the pantry. By the wood-burning stove, she threaded Mary's needle, then watched her sister make tiny, perfect stitches. Laura worked on her own sewing and knitting, but she wasn't as neat as Mary.

When she finished with her chores, Laura told stories and played games with her sisters. On sunny days, she and Carrie bundled up and hurried outside. Hand in hand, they ran and slid on the smooth, icy surface of Silver Lake.

Everyone looked forward to the evenings. Ma rocked

Grace by the warm stove. While the wind roared outside, Pa played his fiddle. For Mary, he played and sang "Highland Mary." He also taught Carrie and Laura how to waltz and polka.

Just before bedtime, Ma turned up the kerosene lamp and read out loud. Laura couldn't wait to hear the serialized adventure stories in the *New York Ledger* newspaper. Each story ended with the words "To Be Continued." Unlike Mary, who was content to hear the next section the following night, Laura always begged unsuccessfully for Ma to read another part.

When winter was half over, a young couple moved into an abandoned railroad shanty near the surveyor's house. Robert and Ellie Boast planned to homestead in the spring.

The Ingallses finally had neighbors. Every day, Mrs. Boast did her chores quickly and came to the surveyor's house. Mrs. Boast was cheerful and laughed easily as she joined the girls in their sewing and knitting. On sunny days, she met Laura and Carrie outside to make snowmen and have snowball fights.

Early in 1880, strangers from the East and immigrants from Norway and Sweden showed up at the Ingalls house looking for a night's shelter and a meal. Some were seeking land to farm. Others wanted to establish businesses—hardware stores, newspapers, banks, hotels, and saloons—in the new town of De Smet.

Unexpectedly, Ma was in the boardinghouse business. She decided to charge each man fifty cents for a hot meal and a place to sleep. Pa bedded their horses in the barn. Laura helped serve the men fried salt pork, biscuits, gravy, and potatoes. She swept up the mud that the men carried in on their boots. Sometimes she washed and set the table a dozen times a day. At night the travelers slept on the floor near the stove, using their winter coats for blankets.

One of their guests was Reverend Alden, a traveling minister who had conducted church services in Walnut Grove. He was on his way to another community to start a new church. At dinner he told the Ingallses about a college for the blind in Iowa. He thought it would be ideal for Mary and promised to find out how much it would cost.

That night, as Laura snuggled with Mary and Carrie in their attic bed, she made a hard decision. She would please Ma, who had wanted Mary to become a teacher. Laura would take her place. Even though she didn't really want to become a teacher, her salary would help send Mary to college. To Mary she said, "I will study hard, so I can teach school."

Carrie, Mary, and Laura in De Smet

FIVE

Homesteading and the Hard Winter

1880–1881

When the snow thawed, the boarders left to stake out their own homesteads on the prairie. Pa began to haul unused shanty lumber to De Smet. Wood was hard to find and expensive because it had to come from the East. Pa owned lots in De Smet, and he started several buildings in town.

The surveyors returned, so the Ingalls family moved into Pa's unfinished building on Main Street. Laura "would rather be out on the prairie with the grass and the birds and Pa's fiddle. I would rather be anywhere than in this muddy, cluttered, noisy town, crowded by strange people."

Because Laura missed the prairie, she drove Ma crazy. Ma decided that Laura should start an informal school in the house and teach Carrie and her friends every afternoon. Laura told herself, "I've got to be a teacher, so I might as well try hard to be a good one." At the age of thirteen, even though she didn't teach in a real school, Laura became De Smet's first teacher.

One day Pa told the family to pack quickly. They were moving to their homestead. There had been a murder south of De Smet. Someone had tried to steal a homestead claim. Pa wanted to protect his property. Laura was glad to leave town, despite the possible dangers, and eagerly helped Ma and Pa load the wagon.

Reaching their claim, Laura saw their simple shanty with the slanting roof that "looked like a yellow toy on the great rolling prairie." It was wonderful to be outdoors and on the claim again. Laura "felt she never could get enough sunshine soaked into her bones."

Carrie, Grace, and Mary helped Ma fix up the shanty and start a vegetable garden. Pa counted on Laura's help in the fields. Although she was only five feet tall, she was strong. They gathered wild bluestem grass to feed the animals during the winter. First Pa cut the grass, then Laura trampled it and raked it into rows to dry. After it dried, they stored the hay in Pa's newly built barn.

While they were planting cottonwood trees for a wind break, a wagon passed by. Laura paused from her digging. She saw two young men in the wagon, driving a matched pair of shiny brown horses with slender legs.

Pa waved and told her, "those are the Wilder boys.... Almanzo's driving, and that's his brother Royal with him. They've taken up claims North of town, and they've got the finest horses in this whole country." As they trotted, the horses arched their necks and stepped daintily. Laura wished she could drive such beautiful horses but knew she probably never would.

Laura helped Pa as much as she could, but an early blizzard swept across the prairie in October, halting their work. For three days, "the wind shrieked and howled like nothing under heaven but a blizzard wind." Everyone huddled near the stove. Ma put Laura to work sewing, never her favorite job. Laura had to pick out almost as many stitches as she put in.

After the blizzard, Pa moved the family back to town. Except for the Boasts, who wanted to stay in their shanty, other homesteaders moved to town. Their shanties with thin tar-paper walls were too flimsy and isolated.

The Ingallses stayed in Pa's building on the east side of Main Street. Unlike Ma, Laura didn't want to live in town. The construction and noise seldom stopped. Wooden building skeletons rose every day. From the windows, Laura saw the busy street and people walking by. She couldn't wait to help Ma put up the curtains.

Houses and storefronts were quickly built along Main Street in De Smet, South Dakota.

By the fall of 1880, De Smet had a population of about eighty people, supporting more than a dozen businesses. The train linked them to the world, bringing news and, more importantly, food and coal for fuel during the winter. A brand-new school had just opened.

Once again, Laura and Carrie went to school. During the first few days, Laura's stomach fluttered. She dreaded meeting strangers and wondered if she would remember anything from school in Walnut Grove.

After a few days, Laura realized she enjoyed school. She started in the fifth reader, and no one could beat her at math. She made new friends. They played together at recess and walked home together from school.

Following supper she studied with Mary. Laura did her math on her slate, while Mary worked the problems in her head. Then Laura read her history and geography lessons to Mary, and they answered the questions together.

A few weeks later, a blizzard hit when Laura and Carrie were in school. Heading home, they held hands in the swirling snow. Sometimes they couldn't see one another. Laura knew that if they took one wrong step, she and Carrie could unknowingly walk out into the open, snow-coated prairie and certain death. Feeling her way along the buildings on Main Street, Laura led her sister home.

Starting in December, blizzards struck regularly. The temperature often dropped to forty degrees below zero. School closed. Between storms, Pa and the other men tried to shovel forty-foot-deep snowdrifts off the train tracks. It was useless. One storm followed another. The trains stopped coming.

To save coal for heat and cooking, the Ingalls family decided to use only one room during the day. Ma stuffed rag

While the blizzard winds howled outside, the Ingalls family huddled near the wood-burning stove.

rugs against the cracks beneath the doors. They went to bed early to save the kerosene that provided light.

Ma insisted that Carrie and Laura continue to study, using her old teaching books. The girls did their school lessons on the table. Sometimes they had to thaw the ink first. Laura recited her lessons for Mary, accompanied by the endless howling of blizzard winds. Mary needed to keep up with her learning, too, so she would be ready for the Iowa School for the Blind.

Christmas came and went. So did Laura's fourteenth birthday in February. There wasn't much to celebrate. The Ingallses ran out of coal. In the lean-to next to the house, Pa taught Laura how to twist strands of hay into sticks to use as fuel. Her hands stung from the sharp blades of grass, but she was glad to help. Laura wrote that "it was a busy job to keep a supply of these 'sticks' ahead of a hungry stove when the storm winds were blowing."

Ma began to fix only two meals a day. She cooked the last piece of codfish. They had no more meat and only a little tea. When everything else was gone, Ma used her coffee mill to grind wheat for bread. Mary turned the handle on the mill or held three-year-old Grace near the stove. Even ten-year-old Carrie helped, but Laura saw how thin and pale she was growing during the hard winter.

Snow nearly buried the two-story building. Day after day, storms pounded and shook the house. Laura twisted stick after stick of hay with Pa. The fire must not go out. Pa's and Laura's hands grew red and swollen. Pa could no longer play his fiddle. There were no more school lessons. They ate coarse brown bread every day. Families began to starve.

Rumors circulated about a settler who had a stash of wheat seed south of town. Pa learned that two young men, Almanzo Wilder and Cap Garland, planned to find the wheat. Almanzo and his older brother, Royal, owned the feed store in town as well as a homestead. Cap was a classmate of Laura's.

Between blizzards, the two men left to find the wheat. While they were gone, everyone in town worried. Laura paced through the house and studied the sky from each window. She gave regular weather reports to Mary. Pa kept checking at the feed store for news of Cap and Almanzo.

With little warning, the weather grew savage again. Ma

used the last of the wheat. At night under their quilts, Laura and Mary talked about the bravery of Cap and Almanzo and prayed for their safe return. Laura tried not to think selfish thoughts about her empty stomach.

Three days later, Almanzo and Cap returned with enough wheat to save the town from starvation. Laura twisted hay into sticks and helped Mary grind the wheat seed for their only food—a loaf of coarse brown bread. And still, "the storm was always there, outside the walls, waiting sometimes, then pouncing, shaking the house, roaring, snarling, and screaming in a rage."

In late April, the blizzards ended. Ice cracked; water dripped. Warm spring winds softened the snow, forming great pools of water on the prairie. Spring finally came, and the grass turned green.

Ma opened the doors to let in the spring air. Sunshine filled the house. Laura was happy. They had survived seven long winter months. On May 10, 1881, the first train got through to De Smet.

Seventeen-year-old Laura

SIX

Falling in Love
1881–1885

After the snow melted, the homesteaders moved back to their land. Pa replaced the tar-paper walls that had been ripped from the house by the blizzard winds. He added two tiny bedrooms and a front room to the shanty. Working from sunrise to sunset, Pa planted wheat and corn. Laura helped Ma start a vegetable garden. Grace, who had just turned four, spent hours in the garden, squealing over each bean as it popped out of the soil, its stem uncoiling like a spring.

In the afternoons, Laura took Mary on walks. Laura enjoyed describing the blooming spring flowers and the shadow shapes the clouds made over the grassy slopes.

Pa also worked in De Smet, doing carpentry work on several new buildings. Laura found a job in town and walked into De Smet every morning with Pa. At the dry goods store, Laura basted and sewed sturdy work shirts. After a day of work, her arms hurt and her neck ached. She tried not to think about the carpets of pink wild roses in bloom on the prairie. By the end of six weeks, she had added nine dollars to Mary's college fund.

During the summer, the family decided to send Mary to the Iowa School for the Blind in Vinton. Mary, who was six-

*Mary Ingalls, at the
Iowa School for the Blind*

teen, would study there for seven years. In the fall, Laura
helped Ma pack Mary's trunk with clothes, a new coat, and
shoes. Suddenly, Mary's last day came. Ma and Pa took Mary
to Iowa by train.

During the first few days without Mary, Laura felt an un-
usual silence in the house. To keep Grace and Carrie from
crying, she made them clean the house from top to bottom.
While she worked, Laura pictured Mary getting settled at
school, meeting new friends, and passing the entrance
exams. Hard as it was, Laura was happy for her sister. She
knew how much Mary liked to study and learn.

Once again Laura vowed to get her teaching certificate
when she turned sixteen, so she could earn money to help
keep Mary in school. She wouldn't have trouble finding a job.

On the Dakota prairie near De Smet, homesteaders were building claim shanties.

Homesteaders were flocking to Dakota Territory, and little schoolhouses were popping up all over the prairie.

For the next two winters, the family moved to De Smet so that Carrie and Laura could attend school. Their teacher, Eliza Jane Wilder, the sister of Almanzo and Royal Wilder, was an independent, strong-willed single woman. She farmed her own homestead north of town and was often too tired to control the classroom.

Laura was happier when she got a new teacher the following year. She especially loved history and writing. She made little books and filled them with verses, such as

> When you open this book
> Just take one good look
> If the rhymes do not please
> You can close it with ease.

In the winter of 1883, Laura was asked to teach at a small settlement twelve miles south of De Smet. Even though she didn't want to live with strangers, Laura accepted the two-month winter term. She would earn forty dollars.

Laura had five students—some were older and taller than she was. Her schoolhouse was an abandoned shanty, and she remembered that "I walked a mile over the unbroken snow from my boarding place to school every morning and back at night." The snow was "blowing thru the cracks in its walls and forming little piles and miniature drifts on the floor and even on the desks before which several children sat, trying to study."

During her school term, she boarded with Mr. and Mrs. Bouchie. From the very beginning, Laura was dreadfully homesick. Mrs. Bouchie seemed to suffer from depression on the isolated homestead. Sometimes she yelled at her husband; other times she was sullen and seldom spoke. Laura dreaded a full weekend in the rundown cabin.

At four o'clock on the first Friday, after five days of teaching, Laura heard sleigh bells jingle outside her school. The sleigh belonged to Almanzo Wilder. He had come to fetch her home. Laura climbed into Almanzo's cutter. He wrapped her in buffalo furs. She hardly knew him, but she knew Pa liked Almanzo and often played checkers with him at the store.

For eight weeks, Almanzo fetched Laura each Friday and brought her back each Sunday afternoon. They didn't talk much during the cold rides. Almanzo was not a natural talker, and Laura felt tongue-tied and bashful. Almanzo was ten years older than she was. Nearly buried in thick furs, she watched his beautiful prancing Morgan horses with their glossy black manes and tails. She stole glances at Almanzo, noting his dark brown hair, dark blue eyes, and "a steady, dependable, yet light-hearted look."

*Almanzo
Wilder, at
age twenty-
seven*

After the term ended, Laura gave Pa her pay. She had been a good teacher, but she never wanted to stay with the Bouchies again. Although grateful to Almanzo for taking her to and from De Smet, Laura told him she did not want to ride with him anymore. She didn't want him for her beau, or boyfriend. Laura secretly admired Cap Garland and looked forward to seeing him and her other friends at school.

Hoping Laura would change her mind, Almanzo showed up at the Ingalls house the following Sunday. Forgetting her earlier words, Laura slipped on her coat and mittens and climbed into his sleigh. Little by little, Laura began to enjoy Almanzo's attentions. It was the beginning of their courtship.

On temperate Sundays, Laura and Almanzo joined a parade of sleighs going up and down Main Street. Laura loved to hear the bells tinkling on the horses' harnesses. She waved to friends. Sometimes she and Almanzo took different routes—out to Silver Lake or north to Spirit Lake, where there were Indian burial mounds.

While crisscrossing the prairie, Laura learned that Almanzo had been born on a farm in New York in 1857. His parents and some of his brothers and sisters lived in Spring Valley, Minnesota. Almanzo wanted to be a farmer like his father. He had come to Dakota Territory for land. Now he was homesteading 320 acres.

In some ways, Almanzo reminded Laura of Pa. Both were gentle men who enjoyed farming. But Laura knew that Almanzo loved horses more than anything else. He owned a pair of young horses that loved to run. They pulled a shiny new black buggy with red wheels. Red tassels trimmed their harnesses.

On some Sunday afternoons in the spring, Laura had to jump into the buggy because the horses wouldn't stop. Almanzo often let Laura guide the horses across the prairie. She knew that Pa and Ma worried, but "it was the most fun I ever had!"

During one of their rides across the snowy prairie, Laura decided to call Almanzo "Manly." Since he had an older sister named Laura, he began to call her "Bess" or "Bessie," after her middle name, Elizabeth.

Laura taught school again in the spring of 1884, this time earning twenty-five dollars a month. She also worked for a

During their courtship, Almanzo and Laura took drives across the prairie. On one of those drives, Laura began calling Almanzo "Manly."

dressmaker in De Smet on Saturdays. Hard as she worked, Laura still had time to play baseball and go to parties with Manly. They even joined a singing school at the Congregational church.

On the weekends, she and Manly were inseparable, and as she told Mary, "we just seem to belong together." Many of Laura's school friends had beaus and were talking of marriage. They were all growing up.

After courting Laura for three years, Manly proposed one summer evening. After they drove home, he "kissed me goodnight and I went into the house not quite sure if I were engaged to Manly or to the starlight and the prairie."

When Laura showed her ring to her parents, Pa beamed and Ma said, "Pa and I haven't been blind. We've been expecting it." Laura knew that Ma and Pa respected Manly and would never forget his bravery during the long winter of 1881.

They decided to marry after the fall harvest of 1885. Laura told Manly she worried about marrying a farmer. "A farm is such a hard place for a woman…. A farmer never has any money." Manly and Laura agreed to homestead for three years. They intended to work as a team, so they discussed farming techniques. If farming was not successful, they would work in town.

In February 1885, Laura turned eighteen. She wanted to teach one more school term. At the time, married women were not allowed to teach. Once again she boarded away from home, earning thirty dollars a month.

The summer before her marriage, Laura looked forward to spending time with her family, especially Mary. As usual, Mary rode the train home by herself and brought gifts she'd made—beadwork, bookmarks, and vases. She showed Laura her slate with a ruler attached to it that moved up and down, and a stylus for writing letters. At times Laura forgot that Mary was blind. Her sister moved confidently through the house, singing cheerfully while she helped Ma with the housework. Laura was proud of Mary's accomplishments at the Iowa School for the Blind.

On the last day of her visit, Mary walked arm in arm with Laura across the prairie while the sun was setting. Laura told Mary that next time "there will be two homes for you to visit."

In mid-August, Manly learned that Eliza Jane, his sister, wanted to organize a fancy wedding for them. But Ma and Pa couldn't pay for a big wedding. After talking it over, Laura and Manly decided to be married quietly before the fall harvest.

On the morning of August 25, 1885, Laura put on her new black wool cashmere dress and a sage green bonnet with blue lining and a blue bow. "Manly drove up to the house and drove away with me for the last time in the old way. We were at [Reverend] Mr. Brown's at eleven and were married at once. . . . Mr. Brown had promised me not to use the word 'obey' in the ceremony and he kept his word. At half past eleven we . . . drove home to dinner. . . . Then, with good wishes from the folks and a few tears, we drove over the road we had traveled so many times before . . . out two miles north to the new house."

Laura and Manly, soon after their marriage. They decided to try farming and hoped it would be prosperous within three years.

SEVEN

Three Years and a Year of Grace

1885–1894

The day after her marriage, Laura rose early to prepare Manly's breakfast and tend to her new little gray house. She was a homesteader's wife now, with chores and responsibilities.

Out in the fields, "the Man of the Place," as Laura called Manly, started his fall plowing. He hoped to turn over about fifty acres before winter. Laura learned to hitch the four horses to the plow. She also learned to handle the plow, which turned a sixteen-inch-wide furrow in the thick sod. After finishing her chores, she saddled her iron-gray pony, Trixie, and went for a ride.

One day, while helping Manly, Laura felt dizzy. She fainted, but the doctor told her there was nothing wrong. Laura was expecting a baby. Over time Laura began to feel much better.

By the spring of 1886, the wheat and oats were tall and green. Manly took out a loan to buy a binder to harvest the wheat. He told Laura they would make enough money to pay for the hay raker and mowing machine he had bought the year before.

Manly plows a field with his team of Morgan horses.

With little warning, a storm blew across the prairie, bringing hail. Hailstones, some the size of eggs, destroyed the wheat crop in twenty minutes. They would have no income until the following year, when Manly could plant and harvest a new crop.

They decided to rent out the house along with some land to pay a few of their bills. On August 25, 1886, their first wedding anniversary, they moved into Manly's old bachelor shanty. It was small, measuring twelve by sixteen feet.

In early December, Laura went into labor in the shanty.

Ma and a neighbor tended to her. On December fifth, after a long and difficult labor, Laura gave birth to an eight-pound girl. Laura named her Rose, for her favorite flowers, the wild pink and red roses that carpeted the prairie every June. She wrote, "A Rose in December was much rarer than a rose in June."

Laura stayed close to home during the winter. At the age of twenty, she had much to learn about being a new mother in addition to keeping up with her daily chores.

By spring, Laura was working in the fields again. Rose lay in a basket with a tiny sunbonnet on her head. Like her Aunt Mary, she had blond hair and blue eyes. A black Saint Bernard named Nero stretched nearby. Nero had simply appeared at the house and taken a liking to Rose. With the big dog watching over Rose, Laura was able to help Manly.

Because of drought, the wheat yield was small. Laura remembered "how heartbreaking it was to watch the grain we had sown with such high hopes wither and turn yellow in the hot winds! And it was backbreaking as well as heartbreaking to carry water from the well to my garden and see it dry up despite all my efforts."

Laura's parents quit homesteading. Pa, who was in his mid-fifties, built a little white house in the center of De Smet, and in December 1887, the Ingalls family moved. Pa became the town carpenter. Carrie and Grace were still in school.

On some Sundays, Manly and Laura took Rose on buggy rides across the prairie. They visited the home folks, as they called Ma and Pa, or friends like Mr. and Mrs. Boast. Following one visit, Mr. Boast asked Laura if she would trade Rose for their best horse. With her heart aching for the childless Boasts, Laura hugged Rose close and told Manly to drive them home.

During the winter of 1888, Laura and Manly came down with diphtheria, a deadly disease. Fifteen-month-old Rose had to stay with her grandparents. Royal Wilder nursed his brother and Laura.

Laura and Manly recovered, but the disease left them weak. The doctor told them to rest for a few weeks. Ignoring the doctor's orders, Manly returned to the heavy farmwork. One morning, he fell getting out of bed. He could hardly walk. Laura took him to the doctor. Manly, who was only thirty years old, had had a mild stroke. His legs were partially paralyzed.

Manly was no longer healthy. Although he regained some use of his legs, his walk was a shuffle and his hands felt stiff and clumsy. Laura had to help him with the chores and hitch the horses to the wagon or plow. They sold some of their land and moved back to their first home, the little gray house.

Like the year before, 1889 was dry. No rains came as spring turned to summer. Hot winds blew in from the south. The winds reminded Laura of the air from her oven when she opened the door on baking day. After a week of wind, the wheat and oats browned and died on the stalks. They lost another crop.

But Laura and Manly looked forward to the birth of their second child. A son arrived in August. Grace wrote in her diary that the baby "looked just like Manly." Everyone loved the new baby. When he was a few weeks old, he suddenly died. The Wilders buried their unnamed child in the De Smet cemetery.

Laura would not talk to anyone about her son. She grieved in silence and cared for Rose, who was nearly three. Rose was allowed to do simple chores, like feeding the kitchen stove with hay sticks. One afternoon Rose acciden-

Rose Wilder

tally caught a stick on fire and dropped it on a pile of hay sticks. Immediately, the kitchen burst into flames.

Grabbing Rose, Laura fled outside and screamed for help. Manly and some neighbors arrived quickly, but the hot winds fanned the flames. The little gray house burned to the ground. Only a few things were saved—some dishes, silver, and an oval glass bread plate.

During the first four years of their marriage, Laura and Manly had suffered crop failure, drought, hail, fire, growing debts, illness, and the death of their son. This time they could not recover. They decided to go to Spring Valley, Minnesota, where Manly's parents lived.

The Wilder family rested for a year and a half in Minnesota, but the cold winters hurt Manly's crippled legs. So they took the train south to Florida to stay with Laura's cousin Peter Ingalls. They hoped the warm weather would help Manly. Laura wrote that they "went to live in the piney woods of Florida, where the trees always murmur, where the butterflies are enormous, where plants that eat insects grow in moist places, and alligators inhabit the slowly moving waters of the rivers. But at that time and in that place, a Yankee woman was more of a curiosity than any of these."

Manly's health improved, but most of the time Laura felt ill in the damp coastal climate. Their neighbors watched them so suspiciously that Laura kept Rose by her side and carried a revolver in her skirt pocket.

Within a year, the Wilders returned to De Smet and rented a house in town. They would both work and save enough money to start over somewhere else. Manly took odd jobs and helped his brother Royal at the feed store. Six days a week, from six o'clock in the morning to six at night, Laura worked for the local dressmaker. Although she hated to sew, Laura could cut and work forty buttonholes in sixty minutes. She earned one dollar a day. It was hard work, and she missed being with Rose during the day. But she knew Rose was happy. In the mornings, Rose went to kindergarten where she learned to read and write. After school she stayed with her grandparents and aunts.

Laura was glad that Rose was not lonely. Pa, with his patched shoes, long beard, and bright eyes, hurried in and out of the house between carpentry jobs and chores. Carrie

The Ingalls family in 1891 (from left to right): *Ma, Carrie, Laura, Pa, Grace, Mary*

was studying to be a teacher, and Grace was in high school. Mary had graduated from the Iowa School for the Blind and was back at home.

Sometimes Rose helped her grandmother sew carpet rags. She learned to knit, crochet, and piece patchwork quilts. To Laura's surprise, Rose liked to sew.

The prairie continued to dry out. Day after day, summer after summer, the scorching winds blew the dust everywhere. Crop after crop failed. Farmers and businesspeople struggled to pay their loans. The banks began to fail, creating the Panic of 1893.

In 1893 and early 1894, the roads filled with people seeking another start. Lines of wagons passed through De Smet. Some carried away neighbors and friends. Laura recalled sad memories of the grasshopper plague and leaving Walnut Grove. By mid-1894, some thirty thousand people had fled South Dakota.

Laura looked forward to a better life in the Ozarks.

Laura and Manly thought of emigrating to New Zealand, where they could farm on a smaller scale. They considered the Ozark Mountains in Missouri and a town called Mansfield, the Gem of the Ozarks. Former neighbors who had moved there sent back glossy brochures with pictures of lush, tree-covered hills, orchards, and healthy-looking stock. When a friend returned with a large red apple, Laura and Manly decided to move to Missouri and see the world.

Manly repainted their wagon and covered it with oilcloth. Dishes, quilts, clothes, Laura's lap desk, a homemade cupboard, a featherbed—everything they owned—filled the small wagon. Laura added a little notebook, too. For the first time in her life, she would keep a diary.

Laura, Manly, and Rose had a farewell dinner with Ma, Pa, Mary, Carrie, and Grace. Pa brought out his fiddle and played a concert of familiar songs. He told Laura that after he died, she was to have his fiddle.

Early the next morning, August 17, 1894, Laura and Manly climbed onto the high spring seat of the wagon and sat Rose between them. Manly shook the reins, and they were off. Holding back her tears, Laura wondered if she would ever see Ma, Pa, or her sisters again.

Laura stands next to a spring in the Ozark Mountains near Mansfield, Missouri.

EIGHT

To the Ozarks

1894–1904

In 1894 much of the population in the Midwest was moving, searching for work. Long strings of covered wagons were coming and going—to Colorado, to Nebraska, or returning to the Dakotas. Others were going to Missouri.

After about a week on the road, the Wilders reached the mile-wide Missouri River. The Big Muddy, as it was also called, formed the northern boundary of eastern Nebraska. A line of horse-drawn wagons waited to cross. When it was their turn, Manly drove the wagon onto a ferry and quickly set the brake line. Wild black storm clouds raced across the sky as he quieted the frightened horses. As they sat in the wagon, Laura and Rose felt the ferry bob in the choppy brown waves. It wasn't long before they reached the other side.

"That's our last sight of Dakota," Laura cried. Tears ran down her cheeks. Turning away from her family, she covered her face with her hands. "Let me be. I'll be all right in a minute. Please just let me be."

Before long, Laura was fine. On the wagon seat, she joined Manly and Rose singing "Oh, Susanna," "The Rattling Wheel," and other songs. They headed south and east through Nebraska and Kansas. Manly tanned in the sun, and his arms grew strong driving the wagon.

Most of the land was bare of vegetation. Dust swirled everywhere, often hiding the wagon tracks ahead. During the day, the temperature hovered around one hundred degrees. Bouncing in their coop, Laura's chickens panted in the heat. Pet and May, the mares who pulled the wagon every day, grew thin, and their ribs began to stick out.

One time they stopped near a settlement of Russians who lived in long whitewashed sod houses. Laura didn't like meeting people on the trail. She worried that some might be thieves or that they might be rude in front of Rose. Manly was more friendly and always cheerful, even with strangers.

Rose complained about the dust in her eyes and hair, and that her bottom was tired of the jolting wagon seat. Sweat and dust lined her face. Her patched calico dress faded in the summer sun. Sometimes she cried that she missed Aunt Mary and the rest of the family.

Laura missed everyone, too, but there was no point in brooding. To distract Rose during the long days, she gathered her close and told stories. Rose loved to hear about the time her mother and Aunt Carrie were almost eaten by a wolf. She also liked to hear about when Aunt Grace, who was just a toddler, disappeared for a while in the tall prairie grass and violets. Rose knew all the family stories by heart and begged her mother to tell them over and over again.

Whenever possible, the Wilders camped beside a spring or river, filling their water barrels for the dry stretches ahead. Manly smashed hardtack, a kind of bread as big and round as a dinner plate, into pieces with a hammer. Laura taught Rose to soften the hardtack by dipping the pieces in tea. They ate fried potatoes, salt pork, and beans off tin plates.

At night Laura pulled out the little wooden writing case that Manly had made for her. The case opened like a book and had compartments inside where Laura kept her paper, envelopes, and pen. A one-hundred-dollar bill, the money Laura had saved from a year of dressmaking, lay hidden under the paper and envelopes. It was their future in Missouri.

By the campfire, Laura wrote daily notes in a five-cent school tablet about their travels. Both she and Manly were keenly interested in everything they saw and wanted to keep a record. To save paper, Laura squeezed three handwritten lines between each printed line. She explained to Rose that "it is like a letter to myself. . . . When our trip is over, I'll keep it to remind me." Laura also mailed letters home. One was printed in the *De Smet News and Leader.* Laura penciled in the margin of her copy, "First I ever had published."

The Wilders reached Missouri on August 22. As the wagon rolled past Springfield toward the mountains, Laura began to whistle, just like Pa. A few days later, she recorded, "Well, we are in the Ozarks at last . . . and they are beautiful. We passed along the foot of some hills and could look up their sides. The trees and rocks are lovely. Manly says we could almost live on the looks of them." Laura and Manly stopped often to examine acres of lush strawberry fields, study fruit orchards, and talk to farmers about land prices.

By August 29, they were near their destination—Mansfield. Laura said that "every turn of the wheels changes our view of the woods and the hills. The sky seems lower here, and it is the softest blue. The distances and the valleys are blue whenever you can see them. It is drowsy country that makes you feel wide awake and alive but somehow contented."

After being on the road for forty-five days and covering

Main Street in Mansfield, Missouri

650 miles, they arrived in Mansfield—population four hundred—on August 31, 1894. The streets bordering the town square bustled with wagons and people. A train pulled out of the depot on the far side of the square. They saw lots of houses with front porches and shade trees. Laura pointed out the two-story brick schoolhouse on a hill above the town.

That night they camped in the woods outside of town. In her journal, Laura wrote, "There is everything here already that one could want." Every day, Manly went to look for farmland. The search took nearly three weeks. On September 24, they put a down payment on forty acres.

For the next few days, Laura could hardly contain her excitement. When she wasn't talking about the land, the year-round spring, or the two-mile walk to town, she was whistling like a songbird.

Laura named the place Rocky Ridge Farm. The property not only had rocks, but steep ravines, thickets of brush, slopes, and heavy woods of oak and hickory trees. The previous owner had left four hundred young apple trees, ready to plant when the land was cleared.

After years on the drought-stricken prairie, the Wilders delighted in the lush green foliage.

Manly drives his team of Morgan horses past the Wilders' log cabin.

A small log cabin would be their home. It had a rock fireplace for heat, but no windows. Laura recalled that "if, for any reason we needed more light, we just punched out some more of the chinking. Light came in that way, but so did the wind and rain!"

First, Laura swept out the spiders and their webs, then the leaves, twigs, and animal droppings. With Rose's help, she scrubbed the new house from top to bottom before emptying the wagon. As they worked, Laura told Rose the story about how Pa had been lost in a blizzard. Whenever Laura paused in the telling, Rose filled in with the next part. They unwrapped the blue willowware dishes and set up real beds. A rag rug, a going-away present from Carrie, fit perfectly in front of the fireplace. Laura set the wooden windup clock and the oval bread plate on the mantel. The camp stove went into the lean-to next to the house. Laura was happy she would not have to cook outside again.

Manly began to cut trees in the woods. He filled the wagon and headed into Mansfield. Long after dark, he returned with an empty wagon and seventy-five cents, more money than he had earned in a long time. He couldn't wait for daylight when he could cut more wood.

Laura fed her hens cornmeal and let them run around the forest floor. They began to lay eggs. In town, Manly traded the eggs for flour and other things they needed. With hard work and a little luck, Laura sensed that she and Manly would succeed . . . at long last.

Over the next few weeks, Laura learned to handle one end of a crosscut saw. She and Manly cut wood all winter long, saving some of the fallen logs for fuel, fence rails, and a henhouse. Manly sold the rest in town by the wagonload. Rocks, tree stumps, root tangles, and brush ringed the edges of future pastures and meadows.

Everyone had chores, even seven-year-old Rose. Laura expected her to keep the wood box by the stove full, set the table, and help with the dinner dishes. During the day, Rose swept the cabin, made her bed, and brought buckets of fresh spring water to the chickens.

Besides felling trees, Laura had her regular chores. She washed clothes every Monday and ironed on Tuesday. Friday, she cleaned the cabin. On Saturday, she baked bread. In between, she did mending and sewing. Laura and Rose picked wild blackberries and huckleberries for pies or to sell in town for ten cents a gallon.

By the evening, Laura dreamed of sleep, but there were other chores to do first. Since Rose would be going to school again, Laura unpacked her schoolbooks. Rose read to her mother from the *McGuffey Reader* or reviewed her arithmetic at the kitchen table.

On Sundays, Laura and Manly slowed down their work schedule. Laura read Bible passages to Rose, or they sat quietly at the table, writing letters home. Laura knew how much Rose missed her grandparents and aunts in De Smet.

The first spring, Laura and Manly planted corn and started a vegetable garden. They dug in the four hundred apple seedlings. Laura thought they looked like fragile little sticks poking out of the barren ground. It was hard to picture how they would look in another five or six years, with thick trunks and a canopy of green leaves dotted with big red apples.

Rose started third grade in the two-story, square brick schoolhouse in Mansfield. Unlike the "town girls," she didn't have fancy dresses and hair ribbons. She was a "country girl" who came to school in patched clothes, barefoot, and carrying secondhand books.

She rode to town on a donkey called Spookendyke. Rose complained that school was too easy. During the long, boring days, she invented a language of her own, complete with verbs, nouns, and prepositions. She called her language Fispooko and spoke it to Spookendyke.

Once again Laura reviewed her schoolbooks. Perhaps she could find lessons to challenge her bright daughter. She encouraged Rose to borrow books from the school library. At night, as her knitting needles created a woolen sock or mitten, Laura read aloud from a book propped under the kerosene lamp. She remembered how much she had enjoyed books at Rose's age and never tired of hearing Ma or Pa read them again and again.

Rose listened, as did Manly. Sitting near the fireplace, he often soothed his aching feet in a pan of hot water while mending harnesses or whittling something for the house.

Rose and her donkey, Spookendyke

Once a week, Laura read the ongoing mystery serial Ma sent them from the De Smet newspaper.

Hard as the farmwork was, Laura and Manly began to prosper over the next few years. The farm was not self-supporting yet, but it provided them with fresh vegetables and a steady supply of eggs. They bought a cow. Manly planned to become a dairy farmer, believing that once more land was cleared, it would provide good grazing land.

Manly also decided to breed horses. He bought Governor of Orleans, a prizewinning Morgan horse. He had always preferred Morgan horses, with their thick necks and compact bodies. Morgans were not only excellent draft and harness horses, but racehorses too. Both he and Laura loved to ride and looked forward to horseback trips around the countryside.

In their spare time, they read and studied about how to grow apples, peaches, and pears. Farming was different in Missouri, Laura knew. In the Dakotas, a family needed hundreds of acres to produce enough to support itself. Here, farming was on a smaller scale.

Each year the apple orchard filled out even more. Between the trees, the Wilders planted strawberries and raspberries. With Rose's help, Laura churned butter and walked into town to sell it for ten cents a pound. Laura continued to sell her chicken eggs and increase the size of her flock of white Leghorns. Bit by bit, she and Manly purchased a few more acres. They felt like they were rich.

One Sunday afternoon, Laura and Manly started to make plans for a new house at Rocky Ridge. The house would sit on a hill under an oak tree. With one braid hanging down her back and her eyes as purple-blue as violets, Laura told Manly and Rose, "It would be a white house, all built from our farm." The house would have bedrooms, porches, and windows of real glass, be unlike anything they had ever owned, and take years to complete. While preparing French toast for supper that night, Laura whistled.

Rocky Ridge Farm was improving, but Laura and Manly needed more cash to make their dreams come true. In 1898 they rented a little frame house on the edge of Mansfield. Manly worked for the railroad, delivering goods by horse and wagon to the residents of Mansfield. Laura cooked fresh, country-style meals for the railroad men. In their free time, they worked at Rocky Ridge.

Rose was eleven when she became a "town girl," but it didn't change her life much. Although she had a few friends, she was shy and seldom invited to parties. Laura recognized that Rose was different. It wasn't hard for her to remember her own school days in Walnut Grove and De Smet, when she loved to throw snowballs and play baseball with the boys instead of being a proper young lady. And like Rose, Laura had been a champion in the spelling bees.

At times Rose refused to go to school. Her teachers were only a few years older than the students and not used to children like Rose, who had strong opinions on every subject. Once she challenged her teacher on his interpretation of a poem by Alfred Lord Tennyson.

Her understanding parents let her study algebra and physiology at home, in the hayloft of the barn. Seldom without a book in her hand, Rose read poetry, English novels, and plays about history and romance. Like the pioneers in her family, she dreamed about exploring faraway places.

Manly's parents came for a long summer visit. They were on their way to Crowley, Louisiana, to live with their daughter Eliza Jane, who had once taught Laura in De Smet.

The news from De Smet was not always good. Pa, who was sixty-six, was suffering from heart problems. A letter came from De Smet. Pa was dying. Could Laura come home . . . quickly? In May 1902, Laura took one train, then another, north across Kansas and Nebraska, into South Dakota, finally reaching De Smet.

With his four daughters and wife at his side, Pa died on June 8. Charles Ingalls, who had always dreamed of traveling west to Oregon, was buried in De Smet, in the cemetery where Laura's unnamed baby lay.

Laura stayed on in De Smet to spend time with her three

sisters and Ma. Grace, who had also been a schoolteacher, was married to Nate Dow. They lived on a farm west of De Smet. Carrie Ingalls worked at the *De Smet News and Leader* as a printer. Like Mary, Carrie lived with Ma. Busy as always, Mary kept up with handwork, church activities, and her music. Most of the time, Laura forgot that Mary was blind. She moved easily through the house, humming or singing softly as she did chores.

Laura had much to think about as she took the train back to Mansfield. A new century was under way, and Rose was growing up. Rose had started her last school year in the fall— the Mansfield school only went through the eighth grade.

Rose Wilder at her graduation from high school in Louisiana

Once again Eliza Jane visited the Wilders. She wanted Rose to join her in Crowley, Louisiana, and finish high school. Laura and Manly agreed to let Rose go to Louisiana for one year. In Crowley, Rose studied history, math, and literature, and also learned four years' worth of Latin in one year. Wearing a white lace gown, she graduated at the top of her class in the spring of 1904. Finished with her formal education, she returned to Mansfield.

Laura proudly hung Rose's graduation picture on the wall and wondered about her daughter's future. Many young women were leaving the farms for the cities, to search for jobs, not husbands. Laura could not picture Rose in Mansfield, especially as a farmer's wife. Like many young people, she complained about the drudgery of farm work and dreamed of life beyond the Ozark Mountains. So Laura encouraged her daughter to learn how to use the telegraph key and send telegrams. Now Rose had a skill that would lead to a job, but not in Mansfield.

With her parents' blessing, Rose took the train to Kansas City in search of work. Western Union hired her as a telegraph operator, paying her two dollars and fifty cents a week.

In 1906, Laura left Rocky Ridge to visit her daughter in the big city.

NINE

A New Career

1904–1915

While Rose was pursuing a career, Laura was thriving as a farmer. She and Manly felled oak, chestnut, and hickory trees, and together they cut and planed them into boards for the new house. Manly hauled rocks for the foundations and fireplace. First they built a one-room frame house near the old log cabin. Each year, the rambling house grew, just as Laura had planned and sketched.

She and Rose exchanged letters constantly. Rose wrote about new jobs and cities as well as her hectic life as a "bachelor girl." It was nice when Rose could send some money home. Laura responded with farm details and descriptions of the house construction, knowing her pioneer days of travel were over. Rose's were just beginning.

By 1908 Rose was working in San Francisco. On March 24, 1909, she married Claire Gillette Lane, a newspaper reporter. They were both twenty-two and full of dreams about success and making money. Rose never wanted to be a poverty-stricken country girl again.

From time to time, Rose and Gillette visited Rocky Ridge Farm. Rose had cut her hair into a stylish bob and wore fashionable clothes. Her shorter skirts shocked the farming com-

*Rose Wilder
Lane*

munity. Once, Rose came to recuperate from the birth of her
only child, an infant son who did not survive.

Back in San Francisco, Rose became one of the first fe-
male real estate agents in California and drove a fire-red
Thomas Flyer. Rose lived a fast-paced life, buying glamorous
clothes and traveling around the country, even staying in the
posh Waldorf-Astoria Hotel in New York City.

For Laura, everything revolved around the farm. Since
1896, when she and Manly had first settled in Missouri,
Laura's specialty was her chickens. She designed an airy
coop for her flock and made sure they had clean water and
fresh feed, grown on Rocky Ridge Farm. Over the years, she

became known in the Ozarks as a successful poultry farmer with the compliment that, "in the winter, she gets eggs, when no one gets eggs!"

Farmers wanted her to share her ideas at their meetings. In 1911 John Case, editor of the *Missouri Ruralist,* a weekly farm magazine, asked Laura to send in articles for publication.

Laura began a new career at the age of forty-four: newspaper writer. Her byline was Mrs. A. J. Wilder. In her many articles about farm life on Rocky Ridge, Laura referred to Manly as "the Man of the Place." She sent Rose a copy of her first article, "Favors the Small Farm Home." Laura's theme,

Laura and Manly (left) *relax with neighbors on their porch.*

which ran throughout her writing, was, "I am an advocate of the small farm and I want to tell you how an ideal home can be made on, and a good living made from, five acres of land. . . . our ideal home should be made by a man and a woman together."

Laura became a regular contributor to the *Missouri Ruralist.* Over the years, she wrote about a variety of subjects—helping Manly on the farm, the overuse of the forests, the role of women on the farm, childhood memories, even some poetry. She wrote a column called "The Farm Home" and later another called "As a Farm Woman Thinks."

Many articles reflected her general philosophy on life. She wrote, "It is hot in the kitchen these days cooking. . . . We would be much cooler and less tired, if instead of thinking of the weather and our weariness, we would try to remember the bird's songs we heard in the early morning or notice the view of the woods and hills or of the valley and stream. It would help us to think of the cooling breeze on the porch where we rest in the evening's lengthening shadows when the long, hot day is over."

Mansfield readers agreed that Laura "knows farm folks and their problems." According to one of Laura's neighbors, "Mrs. Wilder is a woman of delightful personality . . . and she is a combination of energy and determination. She always is cheery, looking on the bright side. She is her husband's partner in every sense and is fully capable of managing the farm. No woman can make you more at home."

Later, she sold some of her articles to other newspapers, such as the *St. Louis Post-Dispatch* and the *Kansas City Star.* Many were addressed to the homemakers, as Laura called farm women. In "Let's Not Depend on Experts," she wrote: "I should like to know who designed our furniture. . . . It must have been a man. No woman, I am sure, at least no woman who has the care of a house would ever have made it as it is. Built-in furniture does away with a great deal of heavy work. One does not have to clean under, behind, or on tops of closets and wardrobes that reach smoothly from floor to ceilings." Laura was especially proud of the built-in cupboards and drawers that Manly had constructed in her new kitchen.

Besides writing and farming full time, Laura also worked on the new house. Finished in 1913, the ten-room, two-story white house had four porches, a library, and a huge kitchen. A meadow sloped up to the house, and a deep ravine was in back.

In 1913, the Wilders finished their new white house on Rocky Ridge.

After years of living in dugouts and windowless cabins, Laura enjoyed the large windows in her house. She could look out of one in the kitchen while she was doing her least favorite chore, kneading bread. Over the years, Laura often wrote about her house, especially her windows. In "An Autumn Day," she said, "I have in my living room three large windows uncovered by curtains which I call my pictures. Ever changing with the seasons, with wild birds and gay squirrels passing on and off the scene, I never have seen a landscape painting to compare with them."

The orchard spread beyond the house. By then, the Wilders owned two hundred acres. In Mansfield and the surrounding areas, they earned the reputation of having quality goods and "following strict business methods." Manly sent peaches, pears, and apples to town. Some of the produce went to other states by train.

Manly continued to breed Morgan horses. He raised white-faced Jersey cows, too, and kept a chart of the milk production for each animal. In general, the weather in Missouri agreed with him, but as a result of the stroke, he would always struggle with his painful feet.

John Case of the *Missouri Ruralist* interviewed Laura and asked how she had time to write. "I always have been a busy person, doing my own housework, helping the Man of the Place when help could not be obtained: but I love to work. And it is a pleasure to write."

Although the farm was flourishing, the rest of the world was unsettled. World War I started in 1914. Fewer people wanted to risk money on real estate. Rose wrote to her parents that her real estate career had ended.

As the war expanded, Laura worried about the young men in Mansfield. She wrote about "our young men" who were enlisted in the military. "The war, the terrible, has been something far off, but now it is coming closer home."

The only good news was that Rose had landed a job with the *San Francisco Bulletin,* a newspaper. At first Rose wrote love stories that were serialized in the women's section. Some, with themes of romance and heroism, were fictional stories based on family life on the Dakota prairies. Within a few months, Rose began to write feature articles about famous people and places in the San Francisco Bay area. She dashed off fifteen hundred words a day on her portable typewriter. One article, which ran for four weeks in the *Bulletin,* was about a daredevil flyer, Art Smith, who did airplane stunts over San Francisco Bay. Another, the success story of actor Charlie Chaplin, ran for two months in the newspaper. Now a big-city writer, Rose earned thirty dollars a week.

Laura sought her daughter's advice on how she might expand her own writing. In a letter, Rose suggested that her mother write a series of articles on raising chickens and submit them, not to low-paying local farm journals, but to national magazines.

In the spring of 1915, Rose wrote Laura a different kind of letter. "I simply can't stand being so homesick for you any more. You must plan to come out here in July or, at latest August. You've simply GOT to."

Laura hadn't seen Rose for four years. She missed her daughter. Manly agreed to stay home and run the farm. Laura made plans to take the train west.

Laura (left) *and Rose walk through the deep ravine behind the house at Rocky Ridge.*

~~~ TEN ~~~

Laura and Rose

1915–1930

Laura had arranged to write articles about her visit to San Francisco for the *Missouri Ruralist*. She would also mail letters and postcards to Manly, promising to be his eyes as she saw the western United States. Manly would save them all, tied securely with a piece of string.

Laura arrived in late August. It was a busy summer. San Francisco was celebrating the Panama-Pacific International Exposition to honor the city's rebirth after the 1906 earthquake. The newly opened Panama Canal gave San Francisco a second reason to celebrate—the city would benefit from improved world trade due to the shortened east-west sea route. At the exposition, which stretched along two miles of San Francisco's waterfront, Laura and Rose visited many of the twenty-eight buildings that represented twenty-eight nations. There were ten palaces devoted to the fine arts and filled with art from around the world. Eighteen million people saw the exposition. Laura and Rose explored festival halls, auditoriums, incredible gardens, and an area devoted to fun, rides, and games.

They walked up and down the hills and saw famous spots like Chinatown, Nob Hill, Fisherman's Wharf, and North

Beach. They went to nearby Muir Woods and across the bay
to the city of Berkeley. After wading in the Pacific Ocean for
the first time, Laura wrote to Manly that "the water is such a
deep wonderful blue and the sound of the waves breaking on
the beach and their whisper as they flow back is something
to dream about."

*Laura and Rose explored the palaces built for the Panama-Pacific
Exposition in San Francisco.*

Rose wanted Laura to see everything. She hoped to convince her parents to move to California instead of working so hard on the farm. Much as she enjoyed California, Laura knew home was in the Ozarks. In a letter to Manly, she asked, "How are the chickens and the pigs and everything? Truly, I am enjoying myself but I am also missing Rocky Ridge. Believe me, I am glad we have such a beautiful home."

Laura met Rose's writer and artist friends. She and Rose talked over writing ideas and worked on stories together. Laura saw where Rose worked at the *San Francisco Bulletin*. As a newspaperwoman, Rose worked with tight deadlines. In another letter to Manly, Laura commented, "I intend to try to do some writing that will count, but I would not be driven by the work as [Rose] is for anything, and I do not see how she can stand it." In one letter, Laura wrote that "I love the city of San Francisco. It is beautiful but I would not give one Ozark hill for all the rest of the state that I have seen."

Manly was happy to see Laura at the end of October. He was impressed with how much extra work he had to do while she was away. Laura was glad to be back, away from cities and crowds. She had missed her Mansfield friends and social activities. Life, she believed, was not meant to be just work, but "a moment's pause to watch the glory of a sunrise or a sunset is soul satisfying, while a bird's song will set the steps to music all day long."

Laura and Manly were active members of the Mansfield community. They often entertained at home on Saturday or went square dancing. Because of his crippled feet, Manly watched from the side, but Laura loved to dance. On Sundays, after church, they rode about the countryside in their buggy. And Manly still drove his horses too fast, especially in town. Once, he nearly got a ticket for speeding.

Over the next few years, Mansfield continued to expand. New social organizations started. Besides embroidery clubs and church-related clubs, Laura helped create the Athenians, a women's study club. The members gave literary programs about the works of Shakespeare, Mark Twain, and other authors. The Athenians also helped create the first county library.

Laura continued to work to improve the life of the farmers in her area. In 1917 she joined the Mansfield Farm Loan Association, as the secretary-treasurer. The association loaned money to farmers to improve their land or buy more. Laura helped prospective borrowers fill out the forms and then interviewed them. Over the years, Laura, through the Farm Loan Association, helped farmers apply for nearly a million dollars in loans.

Laura and Manly never knew when they might see Rose. Their daughter was always on the go—in San Francisco, New York, or somewhere in between. She had divorced Gillette in 1918 and was writing full-time. Using the name Rose Wilder Lane, she wrote *Henry Ford's Own Story,* then her first novel, *Diverging Roads,* which centered around the conflict between marriage and career for a modern woman. She was also writing a biography about Herbert Hoover, who would become the thirty-first president of the United States.

In 1919 Rose came home for a summer vacation, then returned to Rocky Ridge Farm for Christmas. Laura held welcoming teas for her daughter in the parlor at Rocky Ridge. The guests were Laura's friends and a few of Rose's old schoolmates. The parlor, with oak paneling made from trees on the farm and a big stone fireplace, was an inviting room. Three sections of bookshelves formed a walk-in library within the parlor.

By March 1920, Rose was on her way to Europe to work for the American Red Cross. There, she wrote about her experiences for the Red Cross, prepared a series of children's stories for the *Junior Red Cross Magazine,* and sent home articles for several women's magazines. Everyone in Mansfield knew of Laura's famous daughter. They read her stories in *Harper's, Sunset,* and *Good Housekeeping* magazines.

Never idle, Rose also wrote to her family and friends. Every day Laura walked down a hill to the mailbox with one of the farm dogs. She often received letters and postcards

Laura, Manly, and their dog relax in the yard.

Rose sent her parents this photo from Brittany, France.

with exotic stamps from around the world. Laura answered Rose with details of Mansfield life—parties, picnics, and fishing trips—as well as farm news supplied by Manly. She worried about her independent daughter, but she tried not to let her know. Instead, on December fifth, Rose's birthday, Laura held a party at Rocky Ridge. She read Rose's exciting travel letters to her guests, then asked each one to write Rose a Christmas greeting.

Carrie visited Rocky Ridge Farm several times; so did Manly's sister, Eliza Jane. Her family was seldom far from Laura's mind. If she wasn't mailing a letter to Rose or the family in De Smet, she was writing about her pioneer days in her magazine articles.

Rose returned to the United States in 1923. She had been gone for over three years. Greeting her at the Mansfield train station on December 20, Laura was shocked at the sight of her daughter. Not only was she thin, but her hair was prematurely gray, due to several bouts with malaria.

Over the next few weeks, Laura baked all of Rose's favorite foods. Rose took over the second-story sleeping porch and set up her typewriter. She drafted several projects for national magazines. At that time, Rose was one of the country's best-known writers and earned top dollar for her stories. She enjoyed buying her parents special gifts and, at the same time, hoped to save enough money to help them retire.

In the spring of 1924, Ma died in De Smet at the age of eighty-four. Laura decided not to attend the funeral. Although sad, she had many good memories, especially of Ma's steadfast devotion to Pa as they moved from place to place on the prairie. Mary went to live with Carrie and her husband, David Swanzey, a mine owner, near the foot of Mount Rushmore in South Dakota.

In 1925 Rose used some of her writing money to buy a nearly new, blue Buick sedan for her parents. They named it Isabelle. Laura was used to Buck and Billy, horses who pulled the wagon, but she knew that cars were becoming part of the Ozarks. The winding lane near the house was now a highway.

At first, Manly drove the car like a team of horses and nearly crashed Isabelle into a ditch. Laura eventually learned to use the car but let Manly do most of the driving.

Rose (left) *and Laura traveled all over the western United States with Rose's friend Troub.*

A few months later, Laura, Rose, and Troub, one of her daughter's friends, took a trip in Isabelle. They were gone for six weeks, visiting Kansas, Colorado, Utah, Nevada, and California. In California, Laura met some of Rose's literary friends again, which inspired her to write more.

Laura was still anxious to break into the national magazine market. That way, she would earn more. Mother and daughter collaborated on two articles for a popular weekly magazine, *The Country Gentleman.*

In 1928 Rose built her parents a modern English-style rock cottage across the ridge from the farmhouse. A furnace heated the house. Electricity provided power and light. Laura packed away her kerosene lanterns before moving in on Christmas Day. She wouldn't miss cleaning the smoke-stained glass or trimming the wicks. Rose took over the farmhouse.

Although Manly had help with the heavy farm work, he wasn't idle. Every day, he fed the stock, milked his goats, split wood, and tinkered in his workshop. He often drove to town to discuss local politics and play pool.

Laura seldom wrote for the *Missouri Ruralist* any more and resigned from the Farm Loan Association. Since Ma's death several years ago and Mary's death more recently, Laura had been thinking about writing her autobiography. She wanted to write down the stories Pa had told her. At the age of sixty-three, she started to record her family history.

Using a blue-lined school tablet, she filled each page. She wrote steadily for several months. She started with her family's move to Indian Territory and ended it with her wedding to Manly. One morning, she walked to the farmhouse and handed Rose the tablet. In pencil, she had written a first-person draft, titled "Pioneer Girl." Laura asked Rose to type the manuscript and offer suggestions on the writing. As she explained, they were stories that needed to be told.

ELEVEN

A Published Author

1930–1943

Rose typed the manuscript. It needed work, she told Laura, but she recognized that her mother had a way with words and descriptive passages. Rose found it exciting to read the stories she knew so well. Working together, they shortened "Pioneer Girl" into a possible picture book titled "When Gramma Was a Little Girl." Rose sent the material to her literary agent, George Bye. Laura's story was rejected.

Rose, who was then staying in New York, wrote to her mother, advising her to not get discouraged but to play with the text. She suggested that "if you find it easier to write in the first person, write that way. I will change it into the third person later." Rose added that Laura should put back in her "quarrel with Mary about whose hair is the prettier." In the same letter she suggested that Laura "take the book from winter through spring, summer, autumn, and end with the first snow of next winter."

Relying on Rose's advice, Laura changed the manuscript into a story about her Wisconsin childhood for older readers, ages eight to twelve. Rose returned the manuscript to George Bye. Laura didn't expect to sell her book, but she had enjoyed writing about her pioneer years.

On Thanksgiving Day, she received a telegram from Virginia Kirkus, an editor at Harper and Brothers in New York. They wanted to buy Laura's book. Laura was pleased and "hoped that a few children might enjoy the stories I had loved."

Retitled *Little House in the Big Woods,* Laura's book of her Wisconsin memories and Pa's stories was published in April 1932. It had pen and ink drawings by Helen Sewell. The Junior Literary Guild made it one of their highlighted selections. In the promotional material, they described the book and then described Laura, who "is now about sixty-five, small, very pretty and modishly dressed with bobbed white hair. Besides being a writer she is also an expert cook, dairymaid and poultry raiser. Her gingerbread has already made her famous."

Much to Laura's surprise, *Little House in the Big Woods* was a big success. It was awarded a Newbery Honor—runner-up to the Newbery Award, which is presented to one outstanding children's book each year. Laura began getting mail from children. They wanted to hear more stories.

Harper and Brothers asked Laura to start a second book. She decided to write about Manly's boyhood in Malone, New York. Manly supplied Laura with details. Rose helped to edit Laura's text into a year-long story about farm life. *Farmer Boy* appeared in 1933. It was so popular that Manly began to get fan mail too.

At the same time, Laura's young fans said they liked to read about real people in a pioneer setting. Laura vividly remembered when she and her sisters cuddled near the warm stove on a winter night, begging Pa for one more story. Then, Laura heard Rose's voice, too. "Oh, tell me another story! Please tell me another story!"

In Farmer Boy, *Laura wrote about how Almanzo carefully yoked his calves on his ninth birthday.*

Laura sat at her desk in the stone cottage. She decided that her next book should be just about her life in Indian Territory in Kansas. She made notes and an outline. It didn't take her long to realize that her pioneer childhood would fill several books and cover the American frontier from 1860 to the 1890s. Since she had lived in so many places, Laura called her books the "Little House" series.

In her free time, Laura made more and more notes in the lined tablets. She drew maps and wrote to old-timers to gather historical details. She wrote to her sister Grace to ask about the flowers that grew on the prairie. She tried to avoid writing at night, because as she said to Rose, "if I do, I can't sleep.

My brain goes right on remembering." Even so, she often recalled something in the middle of the night and wrote it down. *Little House on the Prairie* was published in 1935.

With the success of her third book, Laura now had a steady but small income in royalties. The news spread quickly in the Ozarks that Mrs. Wilder of Rocky Ridge Farm was Laura Ingalls Wilder, the famous author.

Laura didn't let writing interfere with her daily life. She cooked breakfast for Manly, then did the housework. In the

Laura and Rose, here at the rock cottage soon after Laura and Manly moved in, discussed Laura's writing.

evenings, she and Manly liked to read the newspaper or magazines, listen to the radio, and occasionally play a game of cribbage. They also enjoyed their many friends, church activities, and picnics, but they especially appreciated Rocky Ridge and the passing pattern of seasons on the farm. By then they had sold much of the land, keeping some acreage and the farmhouse.

Laura drafted *On the Banks of Plum Creek* in 1936. It covered the pioneer times in western Minnesota—blizzards, the grasshopper plague, and the first school days. As usual, Laura shared it with Rose. They didn't always agree. Rose had strong opinions, and she didn't hesitate to tell them to her mother. Concerning *On the Banks of Plum Creek,* Laura wrote to Rose: "I have written you the whys of the story as I wrote it. But you know your judgment is better than mine, so what you decide is the one that stands."

Laura turned seventy in 1937. She finished *On the Banks of Plum Creek.* By then Rose had left Rocky Ridge for a three-acre farm in Danbury, Connecticut. Laura and Manly closed up the English rock cottage and moved back into the white farmhouse, which Rose had wired for electricity. Laura had missed the old wood-burning stove and Manly's loving carpentry details, like the dining room cupboards. They never moved again.

In the fall of 1937, Laura agreed to speak at a book fair in Detroit. A friend drove Laura and Manly to Michigan. While Manly explored the Henry Ford Museum, Laura spoke to an enthusiastic audience. In a letter to Rose, Laura told of the children who "want to know how, when and where Laura met Almanzo and about getting married. . . . You should have seen the interest in their faces when I spoke of it."

Before starting her next book, Laura decided to visit the

prairie. She wanted to refresh her memory of De Smet, Silver Lake, and other familiar landmarks.

Silas and Neta Seal, a young Mansfield couple, drove Laura and Manly north. They arrived in De Smet in time for Old Settler's Day in June 1938. Along with other settlers, they proudly wore "Hard Winter" badges to show they had survived the winter of 1880–1881. Many of the buildings, like the schoolhouse, had been replaced. Laura wrote that "everywhere we went we recognized faces, but we were always surprised to find them old and gray like ourselves, instead of being young as in our memories."

De Smet celebrates Old Settler's Day.

Manly and Laura return to South Dakota for Old Settler's Day.

At the Ingalls homestead, Laura noted that "there is a nice farm house in place of the little claim shanty, but the Cotton Wood trees we set that long ago day when Grace was lost among the violets are still growing—big trees now."

They visited Grace and then Carrie, who was recently widowed. Laura commented that "Carrie and Grace who used to be my little sisters are now taller than I am. We talked together of childhood days and Pa and Ma and Mary." Laura and Manly enjoyed De Smet so much that they returned several times in later years.

Back in her study off the parlor, Laura worked on *By the Shores of Silver Lake,* about the family's move to Dakota Territory. Laura mailed sections of the manuscript to Rose. Rose wrote back to her mother, "Silver Lake is good. . . . I am not just satisfied with the lead. . . . it is not written from *Laura's* viewpoint." She added, "Your writing is really lovely. It gets better and better. The only thing I would change at all is some of the structure."

Obviously frustrated, Laura sent Rose a series of letters in January. She did not want "to begin the story with a recital of discouragements and calamities." She wrote: "Rose Dearest, To make the changes you want to make in Silver Lake, it will have to be practically rewritten." Three days later, Laura added, "I am afraid I am going to insist that the story starts as I started it. I was in hopes that I had profited enough by your teachings that my copy could go to the publishers."

By the Shores of Silver Lake was published in 1939. As Rose had suggested, the story starts with the arrival of Aunt Docia, who learns about the grasshoppers and Mary's recent blindness. Despite Laura's concerns, *By the Shores of Silver Lake* was eagerly received and became a Newbery Honor Book.

Every day, Laura walked to her mailbox on the edge of the highway with her brown bulldog, Old Ben. The Wilders owned the biggest mailbox available. Laura received as many as fifty letters a day from children, teachers, and parents. Some were packets from entire classrooms.

Children asked endless questions about Laura and her family. They requested her autograph and picture. They wanted to know if Laura had grandchildren or if "Almanzo still makes pancakes like he used to a long time ago?" Readers praised her books and said they enjoyed the part in *Little House in the Big Woods* when Charles got stung by the yellow jackets or *Farmer Boy* because they liked learning about Manly. To a class of fourth graders, she wrote, "I am glad you enjoy my stories, and I'm sure you are all good children, not naughty like Laura was sometimes."

The Long Winter appeared in 1940. It was about the hard winter of 1880–1881 that had paralyzed parts of the Midwest with unrelenting storms. Laura had planned to end her "Little House" series with a final book to be called "Prairie Girl." Instead, she wrote two books. *Little Town on the Prairie* was published in 1941, the same year that Laura's sister Grace died. *These Happy Golden Years* followed in the spring of 1943. It ends when Laura and Manly marry.

Laura was seventy-six. She had been working on the "Little House" series for eleven years. Although she and Manly were retired, Laura wrote to her agent, George Bye, "that a story keeps stirring around in my mind and if it pesters me enough I may write it down and send it to you."

Laura signs copies of her books.

TWELVE

Finishing Her Stories
1943–1957

Following the end of World War II in 1945, Laura's books became internationally known and were printed in many languages, including Braille. Mail from around the world covered her dining table. Laura answered every letter because "I cannot bear to disappoint the children."

After the war, Harper and Brothers decided to create a new edition of Laura's "Little House" books. They commissioned Garth Williams to provide the illustrations. Because he didn't know the areas, he first toured all the Little House sites with his camera and sketch pad. He even met Laura and Manly in Missouri.

It was a busy time at Rocky Ridge Farm. Besides fan mail, Laura received many other honors. The Detroit Public Library named a new branch for Laura Ingalls Wilder in 1949. It was the first library named for a woman and a living person. Laura didn't attend the dedication but sent two original manuscripts to the library and a special message.

In Pomona, California, the children's department of its library was named the Laura Ingalls Wilder Room. As part of the ceremony, the librarians served gingerbread made from Laura's recipe and hired a fiddler to play some of Pa's favorite

Laura and Manly at Rocky Ridge

songs. Laura sent them the original manuscript of *Little Town on the Prairie.*

During the summer of 1949, Manly suffered a heart attack that left him almost helpless. With Laura's help, he seemed to be recovering, but he was very weak. Suddenly one Sunday morning, October 23, 1949, ninety-two-year-old Manly died with Laura at his side. They had been married sixty-four years.

Rose came from Connecticut for the funeral. Manly was buried in the Mansfield cemetery. Laura decided to live alone at Rocky Ridge Farm with her memories, but she admitted in a letter that "it is so lonely without Mr. Wilder that at times I can hardly bear it."

Friends called and came for visits. Laura baked cookies for the local children who bicycled over to explore the hills surrounding the house. Sometimes the children gathered on the green dining-room floor as Laura sat in her rocking chair and told them stories.

Strangers knocked on Laura's door as early as seven o'clock in the morning. They came from all over the country to meet Laura. She was always gracious and took time to visit with her uninvited guests.

Many of them asked her to write another book. Laura claimed that she was retired. But secretly she had written another book called "First Three Years and a Year of Grace." It was about her early married life. Laura decided to put the manuscript away permanently. She did not want to relive the tragedies of those years or share the sadness with young readers. Without Manly or Carrie, who had died in 1946, Laura just didn't have the same enthusiasm for writing.

During the winters, Rose stayed at Rocky Ridge Farm for several months at a time. Once, Laura traveled to Danbury, Connecticut, by plane. Between visits, mother and daughter exchanged letters. On Laura's birthday, Valentine's Day, and at Christmas, loyal fans sent her greeting cards.

Laura turned eighty-four on February 7, 1951. Nearly a thousand birthday cards, letters, and telegrams arrived at Rocky Ridge Farm. Many were handmade cards from children.

Later that year, on September 28, Mansfield named their library the Laura Ingalls Wilder Branch Library. Laura wore a red velvet dress to the dedication. She piled her white hair high and pinned it in place with a gold comb. During the ceremony, the school band played and children sang to her.

Overwhelmed by her hometown honor, she said, "I can only say I thank you all! From my heart, I thank you."

During Children's Book Week in 1952, she autographed her books and visited with her readers at a bookstore in Springfield. A line of eager children and their parents stretched out into the street.

At last, Harper and Brothers released the new edition of Laura's eight books on October 14, 1953. Laura was thrilled with Garth Williams's work. "Mary, Laura, and their folks live again in these illustrations," she telegraphed her publisher.

The tributes kept coming. In 1954 the American Library Association created the Laura Ingalls Wilder Award to be given to an author who makes a lasting contribution to children's literature. Laura received the first gold medal, designed by Garth Williams.

Although she was in her late eighties, Laura was still active. She did much of her own housework. In the evening, she played a game of solitaire or worked a bit of needlework. A neighbor drove her to Mansfield to shop, bank, and pick up books at the library, especially westerns and mysteries. To keep up with the latest in politics and economics, Laura read the current magazines and newspapers and followed the farm reports. Outside her kitchen door, she always set out milk and bread for the wild cats and turtles who lived in the ravine behind the house. But Laura confessed that "there are days when I lie down most of the time to let my tired, old heart rest."

In the fall of 1956, Rose came home to Rocky Ridge Farm for Thanksgiving. Laura seemed frail. Rose took her to the hospital in Springfield for a complete check-up. The doctors said she had diabetes. Her heart was wearing out too.

She rested for several weeks in the hospital and insisted that Rose bring her spring water from Rocky Ridge to improve her health.

Laura returned home on the day after Christmas. She knew she was running out of time but was determined to live beyond the age of ninety, like Manly. On February 7, Laura turned ninety. She was weak but cheerful. Rose helped her read and sort the thousands of cards, letters, telegrams, and birthday gifts that arrived at the house. It was quiet at Rocky Ridge Farm. Snow blanketed the ground. Laura rested and let her mind drift back through ninety years of memories.

Three days later, on February 10, 1957, Laura died quietly. As her readers all over the world mourned, she was buried beside Manly in the Mansfield cemetery.

Rose closed up Rocky Ridge Farm and returned to Danbury, Connecticut. She had packed Laura's papers, letters, and rough drafts in boxes because she couldn't bear to sort through them right away.

Following her mother's death, Rose began to receive fan mail concerning the "Little House" series. Young readers still wanted to know details about Laura, Manly, and Rose. Like Laura, Rose tried to answer each letter. But so many began with, "Please, Mrs. Lane, tell us what happened next to Laura."

In a box of papers, Rose discovered her mother's little diary of the family's move from De Smet, South Dakota, to Mansfield, Missouri. The diary, she decided, should be published as a small book. Rose typed her mother's penciled entries, then added her own memories of the trip. *On the Way Home* was published in 1962.

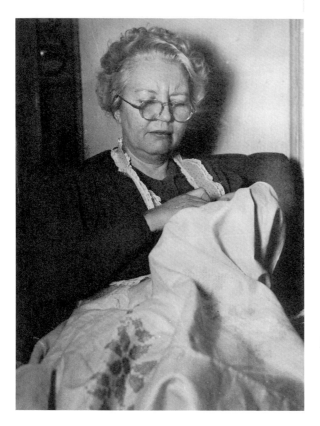

Rose at home

Later, Rose supported the formation of a nonprofit organization in Mansfield called the Laura Ingalls Wilder Home Association. The association would preserve and open the Rocky Ridge farmhouse to visitors and build a museum on the grounds.

Rose continued to write and travel. At the age of seventy-eight, she toured Vietnam as a war correspondent for *Women's Day* magazine. Back home, she studied the globe and realized she hadn't seen enough of the world. So she studied Spanish and planned a three year trip around the world. In 1968, a few days before the start of the trip, Rose died peacefully in her sleep. She was eighty-one. Her ashes lie beside the graves of her parents in Mansfield.

Roger Lea MacBride, Rose's adopted grandson, was the sole surviving heir. He had met Rose during World War II when he was fourteen. He loved Rose like a grandmother. Over the years, Roger had come to Danbury to spend weekends with Rose, to escape the rigors of prep school, college, and eventually law school. He called her Gramma.

Later, Roger became Rose's agent, financial advisor, lawyer, and eventually, her heir. And as the heir to the literary estate of the "Little House" series, he intended to carry on the memories of both Rose and Laura.

Among Laura's papers, he discovered a handwritten manuscript called "First Three Years and a Year of Grace," the story of Laura and Manly's struggles during their early married life. The manuscript hadn't been polished by Laura, and it lacked the sparkle found in her other books. But Roger thought that young readers should be the judges. The editors at Harper and Row, formerly Harper and Brothers, agreed and decided to publish the original draft. *The First Four Years* came out in 1971, fourteen years after Laura's death.

Roger MacBride decided to write Rose's story, which starts where *The First Four Years* ends. In 1993 he published *Little House on Rocky Ridge,* followed by *Little Farm in the Ozarks* in 1994. Other stories were underway at the time of his death in 1995.

Readers of all ages continue to discover the "Little House" series, starting with the first book when Laura lived in the Big Woods of Wisconsin with Ma and Pa and Mary. Laura's books are classics. To read them, one-by-one, is to take a special journey back in time. The memory of Laura, Manly, and the rest of the family lives on.

The Little Houses

Many of the sites connected with the Ingalls-Wilder families are open to the public. There are historical markers, artifacts, and buildings (or replicas of buildings) at many locations. Visitors from around the world come to remember and honor Laura.

To learn more about the sites and their unique features, write for additional information, but don't forget to enclose a stamp. Most are run by dedicated volunteers. They get many requests from Laura's fans.

Laura Ingalls Wilder Memorial Society
Box 269
Pepin, WI 54759

Little House on the Prairie Site
Box 110
Independence, KS 67301

Laura and Almanzo Wilder Association
Box 283
Malone, NY 12953

Laura Ingalls Wilder Museum
Box 58
Walnut Grove, MN 56180

Laura Ingalls Wilder Park and Museum
Box 354
Burr Oak, IA 52131

Laura Ingalls Wilder Site
909 South Broadway
Spring Valley, MN 55975

Laura Ingalls Wilder Memorial Society
Box 344
De Smet, SD 57231

Laura Ingalls Wilder Home and Museum
Route 1, Box 24
Mansfield, MO 65704

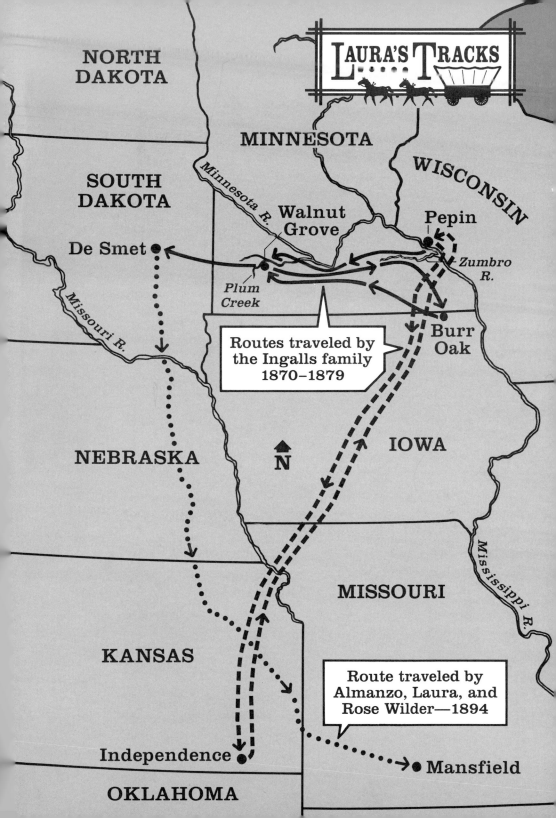

NORTH DAKOTA

MINNESOTA

WISCONSIN

SOUTH DAKOTA

Minnesota R.

Walnut Grove

Pepin

De Smet

Zumbro R.

Missouri R.

Plum Creek

Routes traveled by the Ingalls family 1870–1879

Burr Oak

IOWA

N

NEBRASKA

Mississippi R.

MISSOURI

KANSAS

Route traveled by Almanzo, Laura, and Rose Wilder—1894

Independence

Mansfield

OKLAHOMA

LAURA'S TRACKS

Sources

p.7   "Home," *Missouri Ruralist,*
       August 1923.

p.7   William Anderson, *Laura
       Ingalls Wilder Country*
       (New York: HarperCollins,
       1990), 12.

p.8   William Anderson, *Laura
       Wilder of Mansfield*
       (Davison, Michigan:
       Anderson Publications,
       1968), 14.

p.11   Laura Ingalls Wilder, *Little
       House on the Prairie* (New
       York: Harper & Row, 1935),
       74.

p.17   Laura Ingalls Wilder, *Little
       House in the Big Woods*
       (New York: Harper & Row,
       1932), 75-76.

p.23   Laura Ingalls Wilder, *On the
       Banks of Plum Creek* (New
       York: Harper & Row, 1937),
       111.

p.23   Ibid., 117.

p.27   Donald Zochert, *Laura: The
       Life of Laura Ingalls Wilder,*
       (New York: Avon Books,
       1976), 89.

p.28   Ibid., 96.

p.30   William Anderson, *Laura
       Ingalls Wilder: The Iowa
       Story* (Burr Oak, Iowa:
       Laura Ingalls Wilder Park
       and Museum, 1990), 13.

p.32   William Anderson, *Laura
       Ingalls Wilder: A Biography*
       (New York: HarperCollins,
       1992), 57.

p.33   Zochert, *Laura,* 121.

p.37   Laura Ingalls Wilder, *By the
       Shores of Silver Lake* (New
       York: Harper & Row, 1939),
       19.

p.38   Ibid., 92.

p.41   Ibid., 220.

p.43   Ibid., 254.

p.43   Ibid., 256.

p.44   Ibid., 263.

p.44   Laura Ingalls Wilder, *Little
       Town on the Prairie* (New
       York: Harper & Row, 1941),
       4.

p.44   Wilder, *By the Shores of
       Silver Lake,* 262.

p.44   Anderson, *Laura Ingalls
       Wilder: A Biography,* 102.

p.48   Laura Ingalls Wilder and
       Rose Wilder Lane, *A Little
       House Sampler* (Nebraska:
       University of Nebraska
       Press, 1988), 35.

p.49   Laura Ingalls Wilder, *The
       Long Winter* (New York:
       Harper & Row, 1940), 310.

p.53   Anderson, *Laura Ingalls
       Wilder: A Biography,* 112.

p.54   Wilder and Lane, *A Little
       House Sampler,* 38.

p.54   Ibid., 37.

p.54   Wilder, *Little Town on the
       Prairie,* 200.

p.56   Anderson, *Laura Ingalls
       Wilder: A Biography,* 123.

p.58   Laura Ingalls Wilder, *These
       Happy Golden Years* (New
       York: Harper & Row, 1943),
       246.

p.58   Zochert, *Laura,* 182.

p.58   Anderson, *Laura Ingalls
       Wilder: A Biography,* 123.

p.58   Laura Ingalls Wilder, *The
       First Four Years,* (New York:
       Harper & Row, 1971), 5.

p.59   Wilder, *These Happy Golden
       Years,* 263.

p.59   Zochert, *Laura,* 187.

p.63   William Holtz, *The Ghost in
       the Little House* (Columbia,
       Missouri: University of
       Missouri Press, 1993), 18.

p.63 Laura Ingalls Wilder, *Little House in the Ozarks* (Tennessee: Thomas Nelson, 1991), 62.

p.64 Anderson, *Laura Ingalls Wilder: A Biography,* 136.

p.66 Wilder and Lane, *A Little House Sampler,* 40.

p.71 Laura Ingalls Wilder, *On the Way Home* (New York: Harper & Row, 1962), 27.

p.71 Wilder and Lane, *A Little House Sampler,* 78.

p.73 Roger Lea MacBride, *Little House on Rocky Ridge* (New York: HarperCollins, 1993), 93.

p.73 Wilder and Lane, *A Little House Sampler,* 87.

p.73 Wilder, *On the Way Home,* 65.

p.73 Ibid., 69.

p.74 Ibid., 74.

p.76 Anderson, *Laura Ingalls Wilder: A Biography,* 151.

p.80 Wilder, *On the Way Home,* 97.

p.87 Anderson, *Laura Ingalls Wilder: A Biography,* 176.

p.88 Wilder and Lane, *A Little House Sampler,* 100.

p.88 Wilder, *Little House in the Ozarks,* 223.

p.88 Ibid., 21.

pp.88–89 Ibid., 122-123

p.90 Ibid., 240.

p.90 Ibid., 22.

p.90 Ibid., 23

p.91 Ibid., 250.

p.91 Laura Ingalls Wilder, *West from Home* (New York: HarperCollins, 1974), 3.

p.94 Ibid., 25–26.

p.95 Ibid., 40.

p.95 Ibid., 93.

p.95 Ibid., 116–117.

p.95 Wilder, *Little House in the Ozarks,* 119.

p.103 Rose Wilder Lane to Laura Ingalls Wilder, 16 February 1931.

p.104 Wilder and Lane, *A Little House Sampler,* 177.

p.104 Junior Literary Guild release.

p.104 Anderson, *Laura Ingalls Wilder: A Biography,* 199.

pp.105–106 Laura Ingalls Wilder to Rose Wilder Lane, 5 February 1937.

p.107 Holtz, *The Ghost in the Little House,* 264.

p.107 Wilder and Lane, *A Little House Sampler,* 224.

p.108 Ibid., 225.

p.109 Ibid., 230.

p.109 Ibid., 230.

p.110 Rose Wilder Lane to Laura Ingalls Wilder, 19 December 1937.

p.110 Laura Ingalls Wilder to Rose Wilder Lane, 25 January 1938.

p.110 Laura Ingalls Wilder to Rose Wilder Lane, January 1938.

p.110 Anderson, *Laura Wilder of Mansfield,* 16.

p.111 Ibid., 21

p.111 Holtz, *The Ghost in the Little House,* 314.

p.113 Anderson, *Laura Ingalls Wilder: A Biography,* 211.

p.115 Wilder and Lane, *A Little House Sampler,* 238.

p.116 Anderson, *Laura Ingalls Wilder: A Biography,* 225.

p.116 Ibid., 229.

p.116 Ibid., 230.

p.117 William Anderson, *Laura's Rose: The Story of Rose Wilder Lane* (De Smet, South Dakota: Laura Ingalls Wilder Memorial Society, 1976), 40.

Bibliography

The "Little House" Books

Little House in the Big Woods. New York: Harper & Row, 1932.
Little House on the Prairie. New York: Harper & Row, 1935.
Farmer Boy. New York: Harper & Row, 1933.
On the Banks of Plum Creek. New York: Harper & Row, 1937.
By the Shores of Silver Lake. New York: Harper & Row, 1939.
The Long Winter. New York: Harper & Row, 1940.
Little Town on the Prairie. New York: Harper & Row, 1941.
These Happy Golden Years. New York: Harper & Row, 1943.

Other Sources

Anderson, William. *Laura Ingalls Wilder: A Biography.* New York:
    HarperCollins, 1992.
_____. *Laura Ingalls Wilder Country.* New York: HarperCollins, 1990.
_____. *Laura Ingalls Wilder: The Iowa Story.* Burr Oak, Iowa: Laura
    Ingalls Wilder Park and Museum, 1990.
_____. *Laura's Rose: The Story of Rose Wilder Lane.* Davison, Michigan:
    Anderson Publications, 1976.
_____. *Laura Wilder of Mansfield.* Davison, Michigan: Anderson
    Publications, 1968.
_____. *The Story of the Ingalls.* Davison, Michigan: Anderson
    Publications, 1971.
_____. *The Walnut Grove Story of Laura Ingalls Wilder.* Walnut Grove,
    Minnesota: Laura Ingalls Wilder Museum, 1987.
Giff, Patricia Reilly. *Laura Ingalls Wilder: Growing Up in the Little House.*
    New York: Penguin, 1987.
Holtz, William. *The Ghost in the Little House.* Columbia, Missouri:
    University of Missouri Press, 1993.
Lane, Rose Wilder. The Rose Wilder Lane Papers. Herbert Hoover
    Presidential Library, West Branch, Iowa.
MacBride, Roger Lea. *In the Land of the Big Red Apple.* New York:
    HarperCollins, 1995.
_____. *Little Farm in the Ozarks.* New York: HarperCollins, 1994.
_____. *Little House on Rocky Ridge.* New York: HarperCollins, 1993.
_____. *On the Other Side of the Hill.* New York: HarperCollins, 1995.
Moore, Rosa Ann. "Laura Ingalls Wilder 's Orange Notebooks and the Art
    of the Little House Books." *Children's Literature* 4 (1975).
Stine, Megan. *The Story of Laura Ingalls Wilder, Pioneer Girl.* New York:
    Dell, 1992.
Thurman, Evelyn. *The Ingalls-Wilder Homesites.* Kentucky: Kelley
    Printing, 1992.

Wilder, Laura Ingalls. *The First Four Years*. New York: Harper & Row, 1971.

_____. *Little House in the Ozarks: The Rediscovered Writings*. Edited by Stephen W. Hines. Tennessee: Thomas Nelson, 1991.

_____. *On the Way Home*. New York: Harper & Row, 1962.

_____. *West From Home*. Edited by Roger Lea MacBride. New York: HarperCollins, 1974.

Wilder, Laura Ingalls, and Rose Wilder Lane. *A Little House Sampler*. Edited by William Anderson. Nebraska: University of Nebraska Press, 1988.

Zochert, Donald. *Laura: The Life of Laura Ingalls Wilder*. New York: Avon Books, 1976.

Index

Photo Acknowledgments

The photographs and illustrations are reproduced with the permission of: © 1953 by Garth Williams, renewed 1981 by Garth Williams ("Little House" is a registered trademark of HarperCollins Publishers, Inc.), pp. 1, 6, 15, 18, 29, 34, 47, 57, 105; Laura Ingalls Wilder Home Association, Mansfield, MO, pp. 2, 10, 32, 42, 50, 52, 55, 60, 62, 65, 67, 68, 70, 76, 79, 82, 84, 89, 97, 102, 106, 109, 112, 114, 118; Library of Congress, p. 13; National Archives of Canada, neg. # C-3125, p. 21; Minnesota Historical Society, p. 22; From *The Story of Laura Ingalls Wilder* by Megan Stine. Copyright © 1992 by Parachute Press, IL, by Marcy Dunn Ramsey. Used by permission of Doubleday, a division of Bantam Doubleday Dell Publishing Group, Inc., p. 24; Laura Ingalls Wilder Museum, Walnut Grove, MN, p. 27; MPLIC, p. 37; South Dakota Historical Society—State Archives, pp. 45, 53, 92, 108; Herbert Hoover Presidential Library-Museum, pp. 74, 86, 87, 98, 100; State Historical Society of Missouri, Columbia, p. 75; Corbis-Bettmann, p. 94.

Front and back cover photographs used with the permission of Laura Ingalls Wilder Home Association, Mansfield, MO.